The Religion of Israel

A Short History

by

William J. Doorly

De La Salle House

PAULIST PRESS
New York / Mahwah, N.J.

also from William J. Doorly
published by Paulist Press

Prophet of Justice
Prophet of Love
Isaiah of Jerusalem
Obsession with Justice

Cover design by Tom Dove, C.S.P.

Library of Congress Cataloging-in-Publication Data

Doorly, William J., 1931–
    The religion of Israel : a short history / by William J. Doorly.
      p. cm.
    Includes bibliographical references and index.
    ISBN 0-8091-3705-4 (alk. paper)
    1. Bible. O.T.—History of Biblical events. 2. Jews—History—To 70 A.D. 3. Judaism—History—To 70 A.D. I. Title.
    BS1197.D65 1997
    221.9′5—dc21   97-154
                                                                          CIP

Published by Paulist Press
997 Macarthur Boulevard
Mahwah, New Jersey 07430

Printed and bound in the
United States of America

Contents

Illustrations

This book is dedicated to the memory of my neighbor
CHARLIE (CHARLES) McGONIGLE,
…a friend in deed.

Introduction

There are two ancient Israels, Israel of the bible and Israel that produced the bible. It is our belief that serious students of the bible should be familiar with both and with the relationship between the two.

Major portions of the Hebrew bible, as we have it, grew and developed as the result of competition between two gifted priesthoods in the closing years of the political entity called Judah and in the century that followed. Although the fact is sometimes overlooked, these two priesthoods had a great influence on each other. One consisted of the royal priests of the Jerusalem temple and their descendants, who are now called Aaronids. Scholars trace their origin to the reigns of David and Solomon. The other consisted of a circle of marginal Levitical priests and scribes that traced its origin to northern shrines of Israel, particularly Shechem.

The smaller priesthood, a group that considered itself Levitical, had discovered the value of scrolls in the promotion of Yahweh worship before the official priests of the temple, the Aaronids. Scholars now refer to this marginal group as the Deuteronomic circle because it produced the scroll of Deuteronomy as an introduction to its magnificent history of Israel. Its predecessors may have carried scrolls with them from the northern kingdom at the time of Israel's destruction by the Assyrians (722 B.C.E.). These scrolls would have included the oracles of Amos of Tekoa and Hosea ben Beeri.

When these Levites arrived in Jerusalem around 722 B.C.E., Isaiah was known as a gifted poet of Jerusalem, and his words were preserved in a scroll and added to the Levite collection. The oracles of a social critic, Micah of Moresheth, also drew the attention of the Levites. Like Amos, Micah criticized the decision makers of the capital city, in this case Jerusalem. Like Amos, Micah saw the decisions made in the seat of power as the cause of misery and poverty in the rural areas. (Micah's words are found in the canonical bible in the first three chapters of the book that bears his name).

With the decline of Assyrian power coinciding with the reign of Josiah, descendants of the Shechemite Levites may have cooperated with the official temple priesthood, the Aaronids, in promoting the centralization and standardization of Yahweh worship in Jerusalem. A great reform was to take place under Josiah that would nationalize religion, reduce fragmentation of religious practices, eliminate the influence of rural priesthoods, and put forth Yahweh as the only God of Judah. To support the reformation, the Levites produced a magnificent history of Israel, beginning with Joshua and culminating with Josiah. This history projected into Israel's ancient past a theological unity that could not possibly have existed. It was an ideal created to support the Josianic reformation.

The reformation failed when Josiah was slain by Pharaoh Neco at the Megiddo Pass in 609 B.C.E. and Judah lost its independence. For a short time

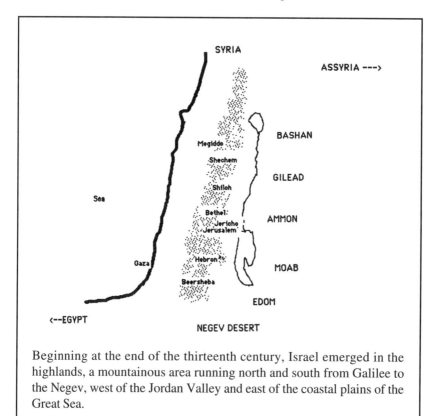

Beginning at the end of the thirteenth century, Israel emerged in the highlands, a mountainous area running north and south from Galilee to the Negev, west of the Jordan Valley and east of the coastal plains of the Great Sea.

Some villages and cities that later became important in Israel are named in the above map.

Map 1. Israel Emerges in the Highlands.

CHRONOLOGY OF ISRAEL/JUDAH B.C.E.

CHART 1

1220	Emergence of Israel in the highlands of Canaan, a hilly, mountainous strip running parallel to the Jordan Valley, from Galilee in the north to the Negev in the south.
1020	Emergence of the monarchy with Saul as king.
1000	David emerges as king, first recognized only in Judah. The northern tribes eventually came to Hebron and asked David to become king of a united kingdom. Jerusalem becomes the new capital city.
960	Solomon begins reign.
920	Rehoboam, son of Solomon, becomes king of Judah. The northern area makes Jeroboam king of Israel.
750–700	Social spokespersons make their appearance delivering oracles critical of the decision makers in Samaria and Jerusalem. Four of these social critics whose oracles have been preserved are Hosea, Amos, Isaiah, and Micah.
722	Samaria is captured by the Assyrians, and Israel (the northern kingdom) comes to an end. Some citizens are taken into captivity, some remain in Israel, others migrate to Judah. Israel had lasted for 208 years.
621	The book of the law (proto-Deuteronomy) is discovered in the temple while repairs are under way during the reign of Josiah (640–609).
609	Josiah is killed in battle with an Egyptian army led by Pharaoh Neco at Megiddo.
597	Jerusalem is captured by the Babylonians (Chaldeans). Many are carried into captivity.
587/6	The walls of Jerusalem and the temple are destroyed by the Babylonians. Judah ends as an independent political entity. Judah lasted for 343 years after the death of Solomon. That was 135 years longer than Israel, the northern kingdom.
539	Cyrus the Persian captures Babylon and proclaims that captured people may return to their homeland. The first group of Judahites return to Jerusalem.

Judah became a vassal of Egypt (2 Kgs 23:31–35). This vassalship was ended when Jerusalem was overrun by Chaldeans, led by Nebuchadnezzar of Babylon, and a period of final disintegration began that ended in 587 B.C.E. with the destruction of Jerusalem and the temple by the invading Chaldeans.

The reformation of Josiah may have been supported by a cooperative effort of the Aaronid royal priests and the Levitical priests, brought about by the agreement that centralization was a worthy goal in the best interest of Judah. If there was some element of cooperation between the two priesthoods, it ended with the death of Josiah. The theologies of the two priesthoods were divergent; they disagreed on too many basic issues. In the meantime, however, the Aaronids may have learned from the Levites the increased value of scrolls accessible to a larger public in promoting Yahweh worship. Eventually the Aaronid scrolls would project Israel's theological past further into the ancient past than the Levites had done in their history.

In the closing decades of the twentieth century, we have learned much about the origin of Israel. We realize that the historians of the Levitical circle (the Deuteronomic circle) and the historians of the Aaronids could not possibly have known the facts concerning the origin of Israel, which had taken place six hundred years earlier. But in their preservation of the traditions of Israel, they have made available to us many clues concerning the practice of religion in Israel and Judah. In this book we will attempt to construct the story of the transformation of a Canaanite population into the people of God by making extensive use of the Hebrew bible to uncover, not the idealization of religious practice, but the historic facts of the past as they are now made available to us. In this book we presume that there was a diversity in Israel from the beginning of Israel's emergence in the hill country of Palestine—nothing like the unity assumed in phrases like "all Israel" and "the children of Jacob." We will review the cultural and theological diversity that contributed to and shaped the development of the Hebrew scriptures by examining the scriptures themselves, a more-than-adequate primary source. We will attempt to sift through the levels of the literary tradition in somewhat the way that an archaeologist sifts through the layers of Palestinian soil, hopefully to uncover facts that will bring into focus the life and thought of our spiritual ancestors.

Part I
EARLY ISRAEL
(1220–1000 B.C.E.)

1

Canaanites, Hittites, Hivites, Perizzites, Girgashites, Amorites, and Jebusites

The Hebrew bible contains two histories of the political entity known as Israel. The first history encountered by the systematic reader is called the Deuteronomistic history (DH) and consists of the books of Joshua, Judges, Samuel, and Kings. The second history was written much later and is found in the books of Chronicles.

The earliest edition of the first history (DH) appeared in Jerusalem during the reign of the Judean King Josiah (640–609 B.C.E.). At least part of this history was produced for public reading. It was produced for didactic purposes and was the product of a circle of Levitical priests with traditional roots in two former northern shrines of Yahweh, Shiloh and Shechem. The earliest version of this history was not identical to the books of Joshua, Judges, Samuel, and Kings as they appear in our bible because the first edition of the history (called the Josianic version) was later expanded and emended to deal with important changed circumstances for the people for whom it was written.

So the Deuteronomistic history started with a united Israel gathered on the plains of Moab preparing to cross the Jordan under the military leadership of Joshua, for whom the first scroll of the collection was named. The book of Joshua is the most influential work of fiction ever composed.

As the book of Joshua opens, we are told that Joshua made the following announcement to the officers of the people.

> Prepare your provisions; for in three days you are to cross over the Jordan, to go in to take possession of the land that the LORD your God gives you to possess. (Jos 1:11)

Shortly thereafter the reader (listener) is given the names of the peoples living in the land to be conquered, who will be driven out without fail by the God of Israel.

...Canaanites, Hittites, Hivites, Perizzites, Girgashites, Amorites, and Jebusites.

Whether this list of the inhabitants of the land was made up by the historian, or whether he borrowed it or incorporated it into his history from another source, we do not know. We do know that the historian used more than twenty sources for the composition of the Deuteronomistic history. Only a few fragmentary sources dated to the period before the monarchy.

Early Israel

For the first two hundred years of Israel's existence, Israel was a preliterary people with no official history, no scribes, and no centralized government. The list of the names of the peoples occupying the land to be conquered appears in the Deuteronomistic history six times (Jos 3:10, 9:1, 12:8, and 24:11, Jgs 3:5, and 1 Kgs 9:20) and twice in the book of Deuteronomy (7:1 and 20:17). Deuteronomy, in several emended forms, served as an introduction to the Deuteronomistic history. We should mention that the list of peoples occupying the land also appears seven times in the canonical (final) book of Exodus in chapters 13 through 34. It is possible that the author/editor of Exodus borrowed the stereotypical list of nations from the Deuteronomistic history, a copy of which was available to the Judahite community in Babylon, where the canonical book of Exodus developed in several steps before it reached its permanent, final form.

What is important to understand about this list—Canaanites, Hittites, Hivites, Perizzites, Girgashites, Amorites, and Jebusites—is that it was a stereotype, a key expression used repeatedly. If the historian borrowed it from one of his sources, it was not a source that dated back to the early days of Israel's emergence in the highlands of Palestine. It has no historical validity. To illustrate the weakness of the list as a historical source of information, let us examine one of the peoples listed, the Jebusites.

The Jebusites

The literary tradition is confusing concerning the Jebusites. Since they appear on the list of seven nations, we first assume that the Jebusites were defeated and destroyed by Joshua and/or Yahweh. Joshua 3:10 states that the defeat of these seven nations would be Yahweh's way of showing Israel that he (Yahweh) was with them, in their midst.

> By this you shall know that among you is the living God who without fail will drive out from before you the Canaanites, Hittites, Hivites, Perizzites, Girgashites, Amorites, and Jebusites. (Jos 3:10)

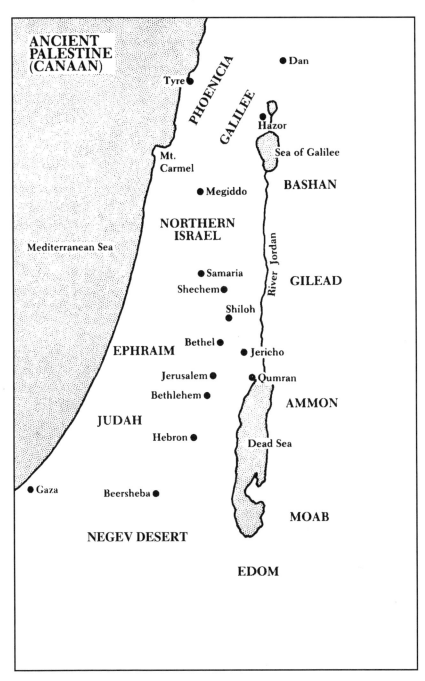

Map 2.

Supporting this, we are given a list of the kings whom Joshua and the Israelites defeated. The king of Jerusalem (the walled city of the Jebusites) is included (Jos 12:7, 10).

Later we are informed of the opposite.

> But the people of Judah could not drive out the Jebusites, the inhabitants of Jerusalem; so the Jebusites live with the people of Judah in Jerusalem to this day. (Jos 15:63)[1]

To further complicate the picture, in Judges we read that it was not the tribe of Judah that could not drive out the Jebusites, but the Benjaminites (Jgs 1:21).[2]

Another complication is the fact that many historians and bible scholars consider the Jebusites to have been Canaanites and view pre-Davidic Jerusalem as a Canaanite city. But in the stereotypical list of seven nations, both the Jebusites and the Canaanites are included, indicating a division between these two people.

The important thing to remember is that these nations were not defeated by Joshua and the Israelites at the end of the thirteenth century or any other time. There was no period of conquest. Before Israel emerged in the highlands between the years 1220 and 1100 B.C.E., the area was largely unoccupied. There is nothing historical about the picture of a united Israel, on the plains of Moab, being prepared for the conquest of the seven nations. The scriptures themselves correct this view of a conquest by a united Israel in Judges 1, where we are told of the struggles of individual tribes and the failure of these tribes to drive out the inhabitants of the tribal area (vv. 27–35).

There was no period of overall conquest by the warriors of a United Israel as reported in Joshua. There may have been a few scattered battles.

The fact that the historian's earliest edition presented a complete conquest suggests that there was a great need to project into Israel's past an initial comprehensive action of victory over its enemies and complete dependence on Yahweh. This need (i.e., to idealize the past) suggests that at the time of writing—the seventh century during the reign of Josiah—Judah/Israel was not

---

During the reign of Josiah there was a need to idealize the ancient past.

---

a united people with a great sense of nationhood. One of the purposes of the history (DH) was to promote the nationalism of the people, and this purpose would be in harmony with the goal of the Deuteronomic circle to standardize and centralize the religion of Yahweh in the city of Jerusalem.[3]

Here are several facts we must keep in mind. (1) The historian, living during the reign of Josiah (640–609 B.C.E.), could not have known how Israel came into existence six hundred years earlier or who the original Israelites were. (2) The historian used a variety of primary sources but had no way to test their veracity. (3) The historian could not have had a modern concept of history, which has only developed in recent centuries. (4) Promoting theology and religious values was more important to the historian than re-creating Israel's historic past. (5) Today, we know more about premonarchical Israel than the historian who wrote the bible history.

SOURCES OF THE DEUTERONOMISTIC HISTORY

CHART 2

1. Song of Deborah, an ancient divine-warrior hymn (Jgs 5).
2. Boundary, territory, and city lists (Jos 13–22).
3. List of Judges (10:1–5, 12:7–15).
4. Stories of ancient deliverers (throughout Jgs).
5. Book of Yashar (Jos 10:13, 2 Sm 1:18).
6. List of top fighters (2 Sm 23:8–39).
7. Stories of the sacred ark (1 Sm 4:1b–7:1).
8. Court history of David; the succession narrative (2 Sm 9–20, 1 Kgs 1–2).
9. Book of the Acts of Solomon (1 Kgs 11:41).
10. Chronicles (Annals) of the Kings of Israel (1 Kgs 14:19).
11. Chronicles (Annals) of the Kings of Judah (1 Kgs 14:29).
12. Cycle of Elijah stories.
13. Cycle of Elisha stories.
14. Military sources.
15. Hymn of Yahweh's unique governance (1 Sm 2:1–10).
16. Historical traditions from various locations.
17. Other sources and fragments, named and unnamed.
18. Prophetic traditions.

Archaeology has revealed that before Israel appeared in the hill country of Palestine in the closing decades of the thirteenth century (1220–1200 B.C.E.) the mountainous strip of land that reached from Galilee in the north to the Negev in the south was largely uninhabited. There was no need for the emerging Israelites to fight for this vacant land.

> *Today, because of archaeological excavation, we know*
> *more about early Israel than the Josianic historian knew.*

We will discuss this in detail in chapter 2, "Immigration into the Hill Country."

A Short Review of the Deuteronomistic History

Before we turn to the historical facts uncovered during the closing decades of our century, we should be familiar with the theological history known as DH. During the reign of the Judean king Josiah (640–609 B.C.E.) a collection of scrolls was produced by a small circle of marginal priests and scribes, a collection that became the first popular history of Israel as a political entity. The history told a story of Israel (Israel/Judah) covering six hundred years. It began with Joshua leading the twelve tribes of Israel into the land of Canaan and defeating *the Canaanites, the Hittites, the Hivites, the Perizzites, the Girgashites, the Amorites, and the Jebusites.* For two hundred years before the emergence of the monarchy, Israel existed without a central government. It is the understanding of the historian that Israel was ruled by Judges during the premonarchical period. In the days of Samuel, who is presented both as a judge and a prophet, Israel obtained her first king, Saul, a Benjaminite.

> *The conquest, in the Josianic version of the book of Joshua,*
> *was presented as complete. (Jos 11:17, 23)*

We are told that Israel wanted a monarch to fight off the threat of the encroaching Philistines and to be like other nations. Following the death of Saul, David became king in Hebron (1009 B.C.E.) and later made Jerusalem the capital of Israel. For several years during David's early reign, the northern tribes refused to accept him as king of Israel. Eventually he was accepted by the northerners, and shortly thereafter Jerusalem was captured by David from Jebusite control and became the capital city of the young nation. In David's old age there were violent fights among his sons for the throne.[4] Solomon, David's son, became king before the death of David in 960 B.C.E. and reigned for forty years.

A great internal political crisis faced Israel following the death of Solomon. At the conclusion of a negotiating meeting held in the northern city of Shechem between Solomon's son, Rehoboam, and the elders of Israel, the northern tribes separated themselves and refused to accept the son of Solomon as their king. Israel became two nations with two monarchies.

The elders of the northern kingdom were able to maintain the name

Israel. (Although it is not presented in this way, it is good for us to know that the name Israel predated the incorporation of Judah into the federation known as Israel.) Also, it may be that the southern kingdom preferred the name Judah, which had been the name of a southern alliance of tribes or clans that had allied itself with the northern federation known by the name Israel. In other words, Judah was a federation before it joined Israel and consisted of Kenites, Calebites, Othnielites, Yerahmeelites, and others.[5]

Following the separation of the northern tribes after the death of Solomon, the nation Israel was ruled by a succession of nine dynasties and nineteen kings, many of whom reigned only briefly. As time ran out for the northern kingdom, kings were replaced by other kings who obtained the throne by assassination. During the reign of the nineteenth king, Hoshea, the Assyrians under the leadership of kings Shalmanessar V and Sargon II destroyed the capital city of Samaria and ended the nation of Israel. Israel had lasted for 198 years following the death of Solomon. Many Israelites were carried away into Assyrian captivity. Other nationalities were transported to Israel by the Assyrians to repopulate the area.

A century later (shortly after 621 B.C.E.) in the southern kingdom of Judah, the first edition of the history that provides us with much of the information we are reviewing (the Deuteronomistic History, DH) appeared. Because Josiah was king when the history first appeared, we call this edition the Josianic edition of DH. This version started with Joshua and ended with Josiah. The Josianic edition of the history was considerably shorter than the version that now appears in our bibles.

Before the Hebrew bible reached its final, canonical form, the history (Joshua, Judges, Samuel, Kings) was enlarged to account for tragic developments that took place shortly after the earlier history appeared.

The early, shorter history (the Josianic history) had been optimistic and full of promise. One of its purposes was to promote the unity of the people of Judah. Its central goal was to centralize and standardize the religion of Yahweh in Jerusalem. The first period of this magnificent Josianic history was presented as a period of conquest. The conquest in the Josianic edition was presented as complete.

> So Joshua took the whole land, according to all that the LORD had spoken to Moses; and Joshua gave it an inheritance to Israel according to their tribal allotments. And the land had rest from war....He took all their kings, struck them down, and put them to death. (Jos 11:23 and 11:17)

The verse below refers to words from the LORD to Moses concerning the defeat of the peoples of the land.

> ...the LORD your God brings you into the land that you are about
> to enter and occupy, and he clears away many nations before you
> —the Hittites, the Girgashites, the Amorites, the Canaanites, the
> Perizzites, the Hivites, and the Jebusites, seven nations mightier
> and more numerous than you...then you must utterly destroy
> them. (Dt 7:1–2)

By beginning this history with a period of conquest that began with the invasion of the land by the tribes of Israel under the leadership of Joshua and
resulted in the destruction of the peoples of the land, the historian revealed one
of the purposes of this history. He found it necessary to project into Israel's
ancient past an ethnic and cultural unity that he believed was needed to meet
the challenges of the age in which he lived, a new age that had dawned in
Judah. For three hundred years the area of Judah and the nation itself had been
controlled by Assyrian military power. Judah and its neighbors had been
forced to pay immense amounts of tribute and taxation of gold, silver, and
numerous natural resources to Assyria on a regular basis and had been kept in
a vassal relationship of restricted freedom. During the reign of Josiah, however, Assyrian power was finally in fatal decline.

This was an opportunity for Judah to restore the golden age of Davidic
rule and to annex the territory known as the Assyrian province of Samarina,
the former territory of Israel, the northern kingdom.

The historian created a powerful concept for the reader (or listener) with
the opening of his history. The concept was that Israel from the beginning had
been a united people, the unique people of Yahweh, children of one family.
There is no doubt that the author was successful in creating this impression. So
convincing was this theological history in creating the illusion of Israel's
ancient unity that it has held biblical scholarship, Jewish and Christian, in its
grip for two thousand years, until the closing decades of the twentieth century.
Only recently—and with some reluctance—have scholars fully realized that
early Israel was nothing like the Israel described in the book of Joshua. On the
contrary, late-thirteenth-century Israel was made up of many diverse peoples.
In reality the author of the Deuteronomistic history had no knowledge of Israel
at the time Israel emerged in the highlands of Palestine six hundred years
before the reign of Josiah, king of Judah.

---

*The author of DH did not know how Israel emerged in the
highlands of Palestine six hundred years earlier.*

The historian uses masterful touches in the book of Joshua to convince
his readers of the truthfulness and historicity of his account. One of these

touches was the providing of the names of the nations (peoples) who occupied the land before the so-called invasion. To increase the vividness of the conquest, the author named the many nations who were living in the area, strong nations whom the children of Israel would defeat with the help of their God, Yahweh.

Archaeologists have for decades examined sites in Israel for confirmation (or lack of confirmation) of the conquest stories presented in the book of Joshua. The central issue for the modern student, however, is not whether Jericho and Ai were miraculously destroyed during the days of Joshua. The starting question is this: Was there a united population called Israel, a strong tribal alliance descended from one family, at the time of the conquest? The answer is no. The fiction is not only in the lightning-swift destruction of Canaanite city-states but, more importantly, in the myth of the existence of twelve interrelated tribes all descended from one man, Jacob, a people who had assembled on the plains of Moab before the battles to hear the magnificent speeches of Moses, the teacher of the law par excellence.

Joshua the person was a functional literary device and is unknown in the remainder of the Hebrew bible except for a minor reference in the book of Judges. The eighth-century prophets probably never heard of Joshua. They certainly did not mention his name.

Joshua the person is unknown in the Hebrew bible after the book of Joshua, except for minor references in the book of Judges. He is not mentioned by the prophets.

The list of nations that had to be displaced by the Israelites—Canaanites, Hittites, Hivites, Perizzites, Girgashites, Amorites, and Jebusites (Jos 3:10)—was also a literary device to promote the unity and strengthen the concept of nationalism needed in Judah during the reign of Josiah, a nationalism seen by the historian as a prerequisite to the annexation of the northern territory of Israel.

This raises an intriguing question. Why did the historian see a need for promoting a strong feeling of nationalism if the people of Judah already had it? The short answer, which we will enlarge upon in later chapters of this book, was that Judah/Israel was always a diverse, fragmented people from the very beginning of Israel's emergence in the highlands (1220 B.C.E.) until the day that the historian presented his political and theological history (around 620–615 B.C.E.). We will explore this diversity by examining the best primary source available to us, the Hebrew bible itself.

Summary

We have said that the Josianic version of the book of Joshua was both fictitious and optimistic. To illustrate this, read the boundaries for the land
Yahweh is about to give to the Israelites.

> Now proceed to cross the Jordan, you and all this people, into the
> land that I am giving to them, to the Israelites....From the wilder-
> ness and the Lebanon as far as the great river, the river Euphrates,
> all the land of the Hittites, to the Great Sea in the west shall be
> your territory. (Jos 1:2–4).

Of course these boundaries were never the boundaries of a historical Israel. Why
were they so grandiose? Our guess is that, with the downfall of Assyria during
the reign of Josiah, the historian was carried away with his optimistic vision.

NOTES

1. The expression "to this day" may mean that Jebusites were found in
Jerusalem during the reign of Josiah when the earliest edition of the
Deuteronomistic history appeared, or it may be a direct quote from an earlier
source that was copied without editing.

2. In the book of Joshua, there are at least two contradictory traditions
concerning the procedure of the conquest. In one tradition the warriors of all
tribes fight together until all the enemies are conquered and subdued (Jos 1:14,
15). In the other tradition each tribe has to fight alone for its own territory (Jos
15:63, elaborated on in Jgs 1:21–34).

3. One of the goals of the Levitical priests of Jerusalem during the reign
of Josiah was to standardize and centralize the worship of Yahweh in
Jerusalem. We believe that this priesthood had its roots in Shechem and
Shiloh, two northern shrines that had a tradition of attempted centralization for
Israelite worship.

4. It is suggested by Steven McKenzie, *The Trouble with Kings,* and by
J. Van Seters, *In Search of History,* that the succession narrative (2 Sm 9–20
and 1 Kgs 1–2) may not have been part of the Josianic version of DH. If this
were true, then the original DH was a more focused product.

5. See Redford, *Egypt, Canaan, Israel,* p. 295. However, in a recent
book by Gosta W. Ahlstrom, *The History of Ancient Palestine,* published
posthumously, the author claims that Judah did not exist as a tribe or a territory
before the emergence of David as king in Hebron, when Judah became a
national term (p. 462).

2

Immigration into the Hill Country

In chapter 1 we discussed the fiction found in the book of Joshua, particularly the earlier Josianic edition of the book of Joshua. The hero of the book, Joshua, is largely unknown in the rest of the Hebrew bible, and no mention of him is made by the prophets, literary or otherwise. However, the greatest fiction in the book of Joshua is the concept of all Israel two hundred years before the monarchy, a united people descended from one person, all members of the same kinship group.

After the book of Joshua, Joshua is virtually unknown in the Hebrew bible.

During the reign of King Josiah (640–609) and thereafter, following the destruction of Jerusalem, when the people of Judah were scattered from Babylon to Egypt and other locations of the Near East, some theologically gifted persons decided that there was a theological need for the people of Yahweh to think of and identify themselves as brothers and sisters, members of one family.

The chief purpose of the original book of Joshua had been to create and bolster a strong feeling of political identity and nationalism among the citizens of Judah. The authors of DH (the Deuteronomistic history) living in Jerusalem during the reign of Josiah had their ancestral roots in the north, and the reclamation of the northern territory was a desired and realistic goal for the people of Judah for the first time in a hundred years. The domination of the Near East by Assyria, which had lasted on and off for three hundred years (900–600), was coming to an end. Assyria was in a period of fatal decline.

> *The chief purpose of the book of Joshua was to project into Israel's distant past a concept of unity and nationalism.*

What Really Happened?

Our task is to uncover the historical facts concerning the emergence of Israel for the end purpose of understanding the origin and growth of the theologies of the Hebrew bible. We have to step aside from powerful misconceptions that naturally result when myth, legend, and valuable functional traditions are blended and presented as historical fact. In the Hebrew bible this blending is done in a masterful and powerful way. Only a constant and determined effort on the part of the student will succeed in uncovering historical fact. There are clues to assist us in this uncovering. These facts in turn will reward us with new insights into the growth and development of the religious concepts of an ancient struggling people whose positive influence reaches forward in time to this day and further.

Archaeology

If the Israelites did not enter into the land of Canaan as a large united force under the leadership of Joshua, how did they get there? In this book we are, as far as possible, looking for clues in the scripture, the literary tradition, that point to valid historical information concerning Israel in various stages of its development. Unfortunately the written scrolls can give us very little historical information concerning the origin of Israel. The scribal authors of the seventh century and later simply did not know the facts of Israel's origin, nor did they have the means of uncovering them.

> *The scribal authors of the Deuteronomistic history did not know the facts concerning the emergence of Israel.*

Today we are more fortunate. Archaeologists, by excavation in Israel, have been able to uncover information concerning the emergence of Israel in the early Iron Age (Iron I, 1250–1000 B.C.E.). In the last few decades of the twentieth century, external data excavated from ancient ruins in Palestine have been able to provide a firm, factual foundation on which to build a reasonable, scientific approach to our understanding of Israel's origin. We turn now to this information.

The Hill Country

(a) Excavations in the highlands of Canaan, the hill country of Palestine, reveal that in the middle of the thirteenth century there were only a few thousand people living there. In the last two decades of the century (1220–1200 B.C.E.) and the beginning of the twelfth century, the population increased by fifty thousand people. By the end of the twelfth century, there were as many as 150,000 people living in the hill country.

(b) Archaeologists have located over three hundred homesites occupied by the new inhabitants in the area being discussed.[1] The homesites consisted of one or more farmhouses (villages). The houses were made of mud bricks, thatch, straw, and limestone.

(c) These farmhouses provided shelter for three or four generations of one family, the extended family of agriculture.

(d) Villages were unwalled, located on hilltops.

(e) The amount and type of pottery uncovered at these villages indicate that "...the newcomers to the hill country were not newcomers to Palestine."[2] The pottery record is Canaanite, not Transjordanian or Egyptian.[3]

The new inhabitants of the hill country were the indigenous people of the land surrounding the highlands.

Immigration from Transjordan?

The book of Joshua has *all Israel* gathered in Transjordan on the plains of Moab for the final great speeches of Moses found in the book of Deuteronomy.[4] Following the death of Moses, Joshua addressed the officers of the people:

> Pass through the camp and command the people: "Prepare your provisions; for in three days you are to cross over the Jordan, to go in to take possession of the land that the LORD your God gives you to possess." (Jos 1:11)

Some scholars, including some archaeologists, unable to shake off the influence of the book of Joshua, lean toward a view that the immigration movement was from Transjordan, from the east to the west.[5] There is little archaeological support for this view. Considering the size of the population increase[6] and the fact that it was gradual, it is more logical to believe that the newcomers came into the highlands from all directions, not only from the east (Transjordan).

The highlands where this population increase took place is a twenty-to-thirty-mile-wide strip of hilly, mountainous land running from Galilee in the north to the Negev Desert in the south. This is a longitudinal stretch of land, frequently reaching three thousand feet above the terrain to its east and west,

---

*Newcomers came into the highlands, not only from the east,
but from several directions.*

---

and is approximately 350 miles long, including 150 miles of southern desert.[7]
This mountain range is divided into four regions from north to south: Galilee,
Samaria, Judah, and the Negev. Each of the four regions is separated by a val-
ley or change of terrain. The Jezreel Valley separates Galilee from Samaria.
The Saddle of Benjamin marks a line between Samaria (Ephraim) and Judah.
The Negev Desert starts south of Hebron, where the land drops. Because of the
harshness of the Negev, this southern area was sparsely populated.

To the west, parallel to the hill country, lies the coastal plains and the
eastern coast of the Mediterranean Sea. The area along the coast north of
Mount Carmel was the location of two important seaports, Tyre and Sidon.
South of Carmel toward Joppa was a marshy plain called the Sharon. The
coastal area south of Joppa became the area of the Philistines, the Gaza Strip.

To the east lies the Jordan River and the Jordan Valley. The Jordan
Valley is below sea level, with the Dead Sea the lowest point on the earth, thirteen hundred feet below sea level. The entire Jordan Valley is the eastern
extension of an enormous rift in the crust of the earth, a gigantic fault, which
stretches all the way from the coast of eastern Africa to Asia Minor.

While archaeology, by uncovering information about buildings and pottery, can tell us certain things with a degree of certainty, it seems unable to
inform us why this population shift took place. And there has been a wide
range of speculation concerning the reasons for this significant immigration
into the mountainous areas. These speculations have included one or more of
the following possibilities: political upheaval in Egypt resulting in decline of a
city-state network; a revolt of Canaanite peasants; development of new technology that made farming the hill country possible;[8] and widespread weather
changes affecting the entire area.[9]

Were the City-States City-States?

The belief that the emigration was a peasant revolt—which has neither scriptural nor external support—is based on a misconception concerning the fortifi-
cations housing Egyptian officials and soldiers stretching along the Via Maris
trade route. In a recent study by Egyptologist Donald B. Redford,[10] it is suggested that the title *city-state* may not have been appropriate. These settlements
were frequently little more than garrisons and walled fortresses. Their purpose
was to keep the trade routes safe and in Egyptian control. While there may have
been examples of exploitation of the non-Egyptian population, this exploitation
was not widespread enough to construct a feudal model for the relationship

*Some of the so-called city-states were little more than gar-
risons and walled fortresses.*

between Egyptians, on the one hand, and the indigenous farmers and residents of
Palestine, on the other. On the contrary, it is probable that the goals and culture
of the indigenous residents, as opposed to those of the Egyptian officials, produced a situation where the Palestinians were just as much a threat to the
Egyptians as the Egyptians were to them. Although efforts were made by the
residents of the so-called city-states to make their lives away from home as comfortable as possible, it does not necessarily follow that the Egyptians stationed in
Palestine could be viewed as a powerful elite against which the scene was set for
a social revolt.

Technology

Scholars have explored the hypothesis that technological advances enabled
the farming community to populate the hill country to an extent not possible
previously. The following suggestions have been made.

(a) The use of iron for tools such as axes and plow points made possible activity associated with forested areas.
(b) A plaster was discovered that made possible the waterproofing of cisterns
for water storage.
(c) An understanding of terracing developed that made level plots on the slopes
available and utilized rainwater effectively, preventing rapid drain off.

It is generally agreed by the majority of scholars that the above-mentioned
technologies developed long after the highlands became inhabited and cannot
be looked at, singly or together, as the sole impetus for mass migration from
neighboring areas.[11]

*Most scholars believe that technological developments can-
not account for the mass immigration into the highlands.*

Where Did the Immigrants Come From?

The book of Joshua has the Israelites entering the highlands from the east.
Modern social theory has the entry made from the west, a movement away
from the string of city-states along the chief trade route, the Way of Horus (the
Via Maris). Considering that the population increase during the twelfth-

century was close to 200,000, with hundreds of sites widely scattered, our judgment is that immigration was from all directions, north, south, east, and west.

Slivers of tradition reach out in many directions. A northern tradition is found in an ancient creed.

A wandering Aramean was my father. (Dt 26:5)

Abraham is said to have entered Canaan from the north, and Isaac and Jacob returned to the north and northeast for their wives.

A nephew of Abraham, Lot, is said to have fathered the Ammonites and the Moabites (Gn 19:37–38), east of the highlands, and of course, the book of Joshua has the Israelites entering the land from the plains of Moab.

The southern traditions are strong. In an archaic Hebrew verse, Yahweh is said to have marched from the south.

> Yahweh, when you went out from Seir,
>   when you marched from the region of
> Edom….(Jgs 5:4)

Moses is said to have lived in the land of Midian and to have married the daughter of a Midianite priest (Ex 2:15–22). And the Edomites are understood to have descended from Jacob's twin brother, Esau (Gn 36:6–8).

While there are no ancient traditions tying proto-Israelites to the coastal plains of the Mediterranean (west of the highlands), we do know that the peoples of the sea, of whom the Philistines are the most familiar to us, took over the coastal areas toward the end of the thirteenth century and fortified their position throughout the twelfth century. The shifting of population at this time in this area, from Egyptian to Greek-affiliated immigrants, afforded an opportunity for indigenous Canaanites to relocate from the coastal plains west of the highlands into the highlands.

It is our suggestion that the new inhabitants of the hill country that became Israel came from all directions. Only this view would account for the large, scattered population increase. Aharoni writes,

> …the hilly regions…became densely populated, and most spaces formerly left open between the various regions were filled….In this unprecedented way the economic potential of Palestine was also increased by cultivation of extensive waste lands which had never been tilled before.[12]

NOTES

1. See William G. Dever, "How to Tell a Canaanite from an Israelite," *The Rise of Ancient Israel* (Washington, D.C.: Biblical Archaeology Society, 1992), pp. 35–44.

2. See Dever, p. 40.

3. See Dever, p. 41.

4. For the Josianic historian, speeches of Moses to *all Israel,* along with the recitation of the law (portions of Dt 12–26), served as a prologue to DH. The Josianic version of the book of Deuteronomy was shorter than the present book of Deuteronomy, as was the book of Joshua.

5. See the discussion of Adam Zertal's view by William G. Dever in *The Rise of Ancient Israel.*

6. The population increase in the area was about 75,000 in the twelfth century and this doubled to 150,000 by the eleventh century.

7. Being a desert, much of the Negev was not densely populated. The city of Beersheba was frequently cited as a southern boundary of Israel, hence the repeated expression, "… from Dan to Beersheba." The distance from Dan to Beersheba was 250 miles.

8. Technological developments considered by various scholars include use of iron for plow points and axes, discovery of plaster to make cisterns waterproof, advancement in terracing, and so forth. While technological developments played a part in subsistence farming survival, no convincing theory has been developed or accepted by scholars to account for the immigration into the hill country in the twelfth century B.C.E.

9. J. Neumann and S. Parpola, "Climatic Change and the Eleventh–Tenth Century Eclipse of Assyria and Babylonia," *Journal of Near Eastern Studies 46* (1987), pp. 161–83.

10. Donald B. Redford, *Egypt, Canaan, and Israel in Ancient Times,* (Princeton, N.J.: Princeton University Press, 1992) pp. 266–69.

11. For example, see an article written by Robert Coote and Keith Whitelam entitled "Social Scientific Criticism of the Hebrew Bible and Its Social World" in the journal *Semeia,* no. 37, 1986, p. 114.

12. Yohanan Aharoni, *The Land of the Bible* (Philadelphia: Westminster Press, 1979), p. 241.

3

Hebrews They Were Not

Now the Hebrews who previously had been with the Philistines
and had gone up with them into the camp turned and joined the
Israelites....(1 Sm 14:21)

---

*A valuable step for the student to take is to distinguish
between the terms Hebrew and Israelite as used in the
ancient scrolls.*

During the life of the political entity called Israel, from the premonarchical
period (1220–1000 B.C.E.) to the destruction of the southern kingdom of Judah
(587 B.C.E.), Israelites never called themselves Hebrews or thought of themselves as Hebrews. The confusion of the two terms for most bible readers—
and for some scholars—is caused by the place of the exilic book of Exodus in
the canon. It is in the book of Exodus that the tribes said to be descended from
Jacob are called Hebrews. Nowhere in the two histories of Israel in the bible
(DH and Chronicles) are the Israelites confused with the Hebrews. Neither are
Israelites called Hebrews in the preexilic prophets.

The Use of the Word *Hebrew* in the Hebrew Bible

A review of the use of the word *Hebrew* in the Old Testament is in order. It
contains some surprises.

(a) The word *Hebrew(s)* appears in the Hebrew bible only thirty-two times.
(b) The book of Exodus, which reached its canonical form during or after the
   exile,[1] contains the most frequent use of the word. There it appears thirteen
   times.

(c) The second most frequent use of the term *Hebrew* is in 1 Samuel. It appears there eight times. Each time the Hebrews are mentioned in Samuel, it is in conjunction with warfare between Israel and the Philistines. One of the appearances of the name is quoted at the beginning of this chapter.

(d) No place in the Hebrew bible is the word *Hebrew* used to identify the language of the people of Israel or Judah.

It is possible that the Israelites never identified the language they spoke as Hebrew. Robert Coote, in his book *Ancient Israel,*[2] states that the language of the court of David in Jerusalem was a southern dialect of a Canaanite language that most Israelites would not have recognized. This language, written on scrolls, became known as Hebrew as time passed. It is possible that most Israelites did not call the written language of scrolls Hebrew, however. We mention this because the use of the title *the Hebrew bible,* which Christians have called the Old Testament, is a phenomenon that encourages students and bible readers to think of Israelites as Hebrews. This is what we are trying to discourage in this chapter.

Who Were the 'Apiru?

The word *Ibri* (understood as a descendent of Eber) is translated "Hebrew" in the English bible. Eber is mentioned in the so-called Table of Nations (Gn 10), but there are many problems related to the historicity of this table. A connection between an Egyptian word, *'Apiru,* and *Ibri* has been made by many scholars, and a review of this term is in order.

Many centuries before the emergence of Israel, a social class of people called 'Apiru, or Habiru (Khabiru), was known throughout the entire Near East. In Palestine these people constituted a semi-independent fringe group— sometimes depicted as mercenaries, often as roving bands of outlaws. According to Egyptologist Donald B. Redford, the name *'Apiru* means "dust makers," that is, people who vacate the premises with speed.[3]

In the Amarna letters, a collection of cuneiform tablets dating from the early fourteenth century, several important references to 'Apiru are found.

The term 'Apiru *literally means "dust makers," people who vacate the premises with speed.*

The 'Apiru are pictured as organized outlaws threatening Egyptian peace in sections of Palestine. In one letter an Egyptian governor of the land of Jerusalem named Abdu-Heba informed Pharaoh that if archers were not sent as reinforcements,

...the land of the King will pass over to the 'Apiru.[4]

Archaeologist P. Kyle McCarter of Johns Hopkins University identifies the term *'Apiru* as a name of widespread use throughout the fertile crescent, only secondarily Egyptian. "It refers to any people in a client relationship with another people. The 'Apiru were hired by somebody else to do something. That may mean military, it may mean household servants, it can be all sorts of things."[5] Dr. McCarter also reports that the term lost its currency in the Palestine area by the tenth century.[6]

Hebrews as a Fringe Group in Israel

The groups that made up the emerging Israel at the end of the thirteenth century can be described as marginal, people living on the margins of a more stable and affluent society. In this case the more affluent society was an extension of Egyptian civilization found along, and supported by, the trade routes between two centers of civilization, Egypt and Mesopotamia. The route more often mentioned is the Via Maris (called the Way of Horus by the Egyptians), a route leaving Lower Egypt, the delta region, continuing eastward across northern Sinai, following the coast of the Mediterranean Sea as far north as Mount Carmel, where it turns inland through mountain passes, including

---

The Hebrews in Israel were a group who gave new meaning to the term marginal. *They were a marginal social class of a marginal people.*

---

the Megiddo Pass and the plains of Jezreel and Esdraelon, and continues past the lake of Galilee and on to Damascus. This trade route, the Via Maris, along with another equally important route in Transjordan (east of and parallel to the Jordan River), the Kings Highway, was protected by a string of walled fortresses maintained by Egypt for the benefit of merchant trade between Egypt and Mesopotamia. These two strings of walled garrisons served as home for Egyptian officials and soldiers who, in addition to protecting the routes for international trade, also provided the soldiery for a military buffer zone against the encroachment of advancing armies either from the north (Anatolia) or the east (Mesopotamia). It was from the margins of this somewhat stable society that some of the Canaanite groups that became Israel moved to the hill country in the latter part of the thirteenth century.

If the Israelites were marginal, the Hebrews who joined Israel were more so. We propose from clues found in scripture that Hebrews were groups of people without land who supported themselves by entering into contracts with stable populations. They supported themselves as farm workers, mercenaries, and in the case of Egypt, builders (for builders read laborers). In the verse at the beginning of this chapter, we read of "...the Hebrews who previously had been with the Philistines." In this reference we have an example of a group of Hebrews employed as mercenaries.

It is intriguing to consider, if the above information is correct, that it may have been a group of Hebrews, people on the lowest wrung of the social

---

The bible portrays Yahweh as a God of war who came from the southern regions of Palestine.

---

ladder, that introduced the worship of Yahweh into northern Israel. Groups of Hebrews became aware of Yahweh in their travels in Midian and southern Palestine, where archaic Hebrew poetry locates the earliest references to Yahweh. It was in this area, the bible tells us, that Yahweh first revealed his name to Moses (Ex 3:13–16). In the following early verse Yahweh is located south of Palestine and in the area of Sinai.

> Yahweh, when you went out of Seir,
>   when you marched from the region of Edom,
>   the earth trembled,
> and the heavens poured,
>   the clouds indeed poured water.
> The mountains quaked before the One of Sinai,
> before Yahweh, the God Israel. (Jgs 5:4–5)

It is not unreasonable to believe that the core of the Egyptian exodus experience was the factual experience of a group of Hebrew laborers who tried to leave Egypt at the end of a contract period and were forbidden, resulting in captivity and virtual imprisonment. These Hebrews were able to escape by calling on their god, Yahweh, who was a warrior god that championed the cause of powerless people:

> Yahweh was a man of war; (Ex 15:3)
> Yahweh will fight for you and you have only to be still; (Ex 14:14)
> The LORD God who goes before you will himself fight
> for you. (Dt 1:30)

When these Hebrews later reached the hill country of Palestine, they became part of Israel and enthusiastically boasted of the victory of their god over the great power of Egypt.

The original Israelites were mostly Canaanites (see chapter 2), and the original God of Israel was El, as the name Israel indicates. El was a high god of the Canaanite pantheon; Asherah was his consort. A particular group of Hebrews, in their enthusiasm for Yahweh, would have been able to make a strong case for the adoption of Yahweh as a fitting god for the clans in Israel with which they (Hebrews) came in contact, as opposed to El, or in addition to El, who was the god of the status quo, a god of the people from whom an emerging Israel was separating itself.

NOTES

1. Scholars agree that the book of Exodus reached its final form as a result of sixth-century redaction and credit P (the Priestly source) as the final author. There is no doubt, however, that ancient sources were used. It is our belief that an ancient source for the exodus experience was built around a factual experience of a group of Hebrews.

2. Robert Coote, *Early Israel* (Minneapolis: Fortress Press, 1990). Coote says the village population of Palestine spoke dialects of the Canaanite language and Aramaic. The urban population throughout the entire history of biblical Israel spoke more than twenty languages (p. 25). He writes later in the book, "The Hebrew used in David's court was a southern variety that only a small minority of Israelites would have recognized as their own" (p. 160). In Isaiah 36:11 and 2 Kings 20:26 the language of Jerusalem is not referred to as Hebrew but "...the language of Judah."

3. Donald B. Redford, *Egypt, Canaan, and Israel in Ancient Times* (Princeton, N.J.: Princeton University Press, 1992), p. 195.

4. *The Ancient Near East,* Vol. 1: *An Anthology of Text and Pictures* (Princeton, N.J.: Princeton University Press, 1958), James B. Pritchard, ed., p. 274.

5. Dr. McCarter made these remarks during a question-and-answer period at the Smithsonian Institute as a panel member of an October 26, 1991, symposium sponsored by the Resident Associate Program and published by the Biblical Archaeology Society, Washington D.C., 1992.

6. *The Rise of Ancient Israel* (Washington, D.C.: Biblical Archaeology Society, 1992), p. 99.

4

The Strange Unevenness
of the Book of Judges

> So the Israelites lived among the Canaanites, the Hittites, the
> Amorites, the Perizzites, the Hivites, and the Jebusites; and they
> took their daughters as wives for themselves, and their own
> daughters they gave to their sons. (Jgs 3:5–6)[1]

The book of Joshua accomplished the purpose of the historian. The idealization of an original political and religious unity of Israel, projected into the
ancient past by the book of Joshua, is so powerful that the student/reader of the
bible is frequently unaware that this unity, described by the simple phrase "all
Israel," is totally lacking in the book of Judges.

The first chapter of Judges was not part of the original book and is not
found in some ancient Hebrew manuscripts.[2] In Joshua all the tribes were com-

---

*Judges, chapter 1, challenges "...the oversimplified view of
a rapid conquest by united Israel as set forth in Joshua 1–12
and presupposed by division of conquered Canaan among
the tribes in chapters 13–21."*[3]

---

manded to assist individual tribes (your kindred) in the complete conquest of
the land.

> ...all the warriors among you shall cross over armed before your
> kindred and shall help them, until the LORD gives rest to your kin-
> dred as well as to you, and they too take possession of the land that
> the LORD your God is giving them. (Jos 1:14–15)

29

In Judges 1 cooperation between the tribes disappears. Individual tribes, fighting alone, are said repeatedly to be unable to subdue the area assigned to them. For example:

> Naphtali did not drive out the inhabitants of Beth-shemesh, or the inhabitants of Beth-anath, but lived among the Canaanites, the inhabitants of the land. (Jgs 1:33)

In Judges 1 each tribe fights for its own territory.

The concluding verse of the book of Judges summarizes a lack of unity.

> ...all the people did what was right in their own eyes. (Jgs 21:25)

The book of Judges served a different purpose for the historian. The original book was a collection of ancient hero stories gathered from various locations (local traditions). These stories provide invaluable material for students of folklore. By stringing these ancient stories together, the historian was able to account for the passage of time from the conquest to the introduction of Samuel, a key figure in DH. Samuel was a judge, a prophet, a priest, and a theologian. He would serve as a prophet who would play a vital role in beginning the era of the monarchy.

The Office of Judge

The historian was aware that before the appearance of Samuel on the stage of Israel's history, there was in Israel an office called a judge. Available to the historian was a list of judges (it appears in chapter 10:1–5 and continues in chapter 12:7–15). The only name from the collection of ancient hero stories to appear in this list of judges is Jephthah. The combining of the ancient hero stories with the concept of judge, an administrative position of responsibility that required great wisdom, produced at best an awkward end product (the book of Judges) that puzzles the modern reader.

Combining ancient hero stories with the concept of judges produced an awkward end product.

No Mention of the Book of the Law in Judges

More puzzling, however, is the complete absence in the book of Judges of any mention of the Book of the Law *(sepher hatorah)*. In Joshua, the Book of the Law plays a primary and central role.

> This book of the law shall not depart out of your mouth: you shall meditate on it day and night, so that you may be careful to act in accordance with all that is written in it. (Jos 1:8)

And again,

> And afterward he (Joshua) read all the words of the law....There was not a word of all that Moses commanded that Joshua did not read before all the assembly of Israel. (Jos 8:34–35)

In the Josianic edition of the book of Judges, the author(s) of the Deuteronomistic history (DH) did not present a picture of Yahweh as a God preoccupied with a written code of law. This fact, along with the real possibility that the slight references to both Moses and Joshua in Judges may have been late editorial insertions (redaction), lends support to the consideration that the main purpose of the original book of Judges was simply to use a string of ancient stories to move the history along, providing a bridge between the conquest and the dawn of the monarchical age introduced by the activity of Samuel.

The Four-Part Theological Pattern of Judges

There is a four-part pattern (sin-punishment-repentance-deliverance), repeated again and again in the book of Judges, with which all readers are familiar. A clear example of this pattern is found in Judges 3:7–11.[4]

(a) "The Israelites did what was evil in the sight of the LORD." (v. 7)
(b) "The anger of the LORD was kindled against Israel." (v. 8)
(c) "...the Israelites cried out to the LORD." (v. 9)
(d) "the LORD raised up a deliverer for Israel....the land had rest." (vv. 9 and 11)

Above, we have suggested that in the Josianic edition the ancient stories (primary sources) may only have served the purpose of moving the history of the people forward to the days of Samuel when the monarchy was established.

> *The repeated four-part theological motif in the book of Judges can be summed up in four words: sin, punishment, repentance, deliverance.*

An examination of the theology of the four-part theological pattern supports this suggestion. The punishment comes from Yahweh as a result of the behavior of the people. It blames the people of Yahweh for the terrible situation in which they find themselves and gives them hope, encouraging them to

"...cry to the LORD," who in times past sent salvation and restored rest to the land. The emphasis on repentance and ultimate deliverance based on the mercy of Yahweh presents theological views prevalent during the period of Judah's scattering following the complete destruction of Jerusalem and the temple by the Babylonians. For this reason we believe that the four-part theo-

---

The theological themes of repentance and the mercy of Yahweh are at home during the period of the exile.

---

logical pattern was superimposed on the string of stories in Judges, which, in its earliest version, only served the practical purpose of moving the history from the conquest period to the appearance of Samuel. With the appearance of Samuel, the theme of the unity of ancient Israel (ignored in the book of Judges) was reintroduced.

> And *all Israel* from Dan to Beersheba knew that Samuel was a trustworthy prophet of the LORD. (1 Sm 3:20)

NOTES

1. In this passage, as in other biblical passages, intermarriage between Israelites and others is mentioned as a matter of information without condemnation. Intermarriage became an issue for Judahites late in the Babylonian captivity and during the postexilic period.

2. The Septuagint, an early Greek translation of the Hebrew bible, did not include the opening chapter of Judges. See P. Kyle McCarter, Jr., "The Origins of Israelite Religion," *The Rise of Ancient Israel*, pp. 120–21.

3. Norman Gottwald, *The Hebrew Bible, A Socio-Literary Introduction*, p. 236.

4. Some scholars divide the pattern into six steps (sin, punishment, call for help, raising up of the judge, victory, and peace. See p. 377 of *Reading the Old Testament* by Lawrence Boadt.

5

The Myth of the Twelve Tribes

> When the entire nation had finished crossing over the Jordan, the
> LORD said to Joshua: Select twelve men from the people, one from
> each tribe. (Jos 4:1–2)

There is no doubt that by the reign of Josiah (640–609 B.C.E.), when the above
words were written, the belief that Israel began as twelve tribes descended
from the twelve sons of one man, Jacob, was widespread in Judah. There was
no historical basis for this attractive and oversimplified concept, however.
This convenient folkloric concept appeared early in the monarchy, probably
during the reign of David, and no later than the reign of Solomon.

The Scroll of the Yahwist (J)

The tradition of the twelve tribes of Israel first appeared in the literature of
Israel during the reign of David. This tradition was the work of the most creative author of the Hebrew bible. We do not know his name. He is widely
referred to in the world of scholarship by one letter, J.[1] He is frequently called
the Yahwist. He may have borrowed the names of the sons of Jacob from an
administrative plan developed by and for David to unite areas of the land that
David identified as his kingdom. Robert and Mary Coote suggest that J may
have "…used tribal nomenclature and copied David's twelve-tribe structure of
administration in order to foster the integration of tribes like Judah with (the
rest of) Israel."[2]

The J document was produced for a limited audience, those whom
David considered the influential and powerful, whose support he needed.
While we do not have information about the circulation or popularity of the J
document, it is possible that its content never reached the masses of Israel. The

Cootes write, "Only a tiny fraction of David's subjects knew or cared what it (the J document) said."[3]

Three centuries later, during the reign of Josiah, Levitical scribes producing the Josianic version of the Deuteronomic history would identify the names of the twelve tribes who gathered at Mount Ebal and Mount Gerazim for the blessings and curses by using the names that appeared in the J document.[4]

Were There Tribes in Premonarchic Israel?

The tradition of tribal organization and structure in the writings of J and, later, in the Deuteronomistic history is so artful and so powerful that it is difficult for students and scholars to imagine a premonarchic Israel without tribes. Is it possible that during the premonarchic period there was no widespread understanding or awareness among the people of Israel that there was such a thing as tribal structure? It certainly is possible to believe that the number twelve had no special significance for the loose federation of highland villages.

Before the monarchy, strong social institutions made life possible for the farming families of the highlands.

Before the coming of the monarchy, strong functional social institutions emerged in an uncentralized Israel. It would not have been possible for the thousands of families making up the people Israel to have survived without the development of strong social institutions.

The basic producing and consuming unit of society was the family, the *beth-av,* or "house of the father." This was the extended, intergenerational family of agriculture. All members of the *beth-av,* consisting of three and sometimes four generations, lived together. All members of the families contributed to the survival of the family. The families of Israel were subsistence farmers; they were free farmers. By this we mean two things: (a) The families farmed their own land; they were not tenant farmers. And (b) they kept the produce of their labor. This does not mean that they consumed all of their crops. Produce not needed for consumption could be shared, bartered, or stored.

Although we have referred to the farming families of proto-Israel as marginal, they should not be viewed as ignorant peasants. Successful subsistence farming in the fragile area we know as the highlands took a high degree of skill, knowledge, and perseverance. That these families were able to support themselves for two centuries proves that they were on the cutting edge of agricultural technology. Although they were part of a preliterate society, we should be careful not to underestimate their understanding and their shrewdness.

The families of proto-Israel were on the cutting edge of farming technology.

Families had a need for cooperation with other nearby families, and the scriptures give us evidence of groups of families forming a unit called the *mishpahah.*[5] Within the *mishpahah* families were not only able to share surpluses, they were also able to optimize labor and participate in labor-intensive community projects such as the construction of cisterns, terraces, threshing floors, and storage facilities.[6] Nonagricultural projects would include well digging and defense works.

Although the Hebrew word *mishpahah* is often translated "clan," Norman Gottwald, in his classic work *The Tribes of Yahweh,* explains why the *mishpahah* was not a clan in the strict sense of the word.

> ...in a clan-organized society, the family is decisively subordinated and circumscribed by the clan. Families constellate through marriage and birth and dissolve through divorce and death, while the clan structure goes on in functional perpetuity....indeed the family looks like the clan's reproductive agency, so located in relation to the clan that it performs its limited functions without threatening the ever-renewed power base of the clan.[7]

The *mishpahah* was not a clan. It did not dominate the family. It came into existence for the purpose of preserving the family. If circumstances threatened the existence of the family, the *mishpahah* would be there to rescue it and insure its continuance. For this reason Gottwald defines the *mishpahah* as a "protective association of extended families."[8]

If the tribe existed, it was the weakest of the primary social institutions. Perhaps tribes were defined by geography and consisted of the family alliances ("clans" in the NRSV and other English translations) and households living in contiguous areas. The purpose of a tribe may have been loosely related to a military-like organization for defense against hostile groups that, from time to time, had designs on the land area occupied by the farmers of Israel.

How Many Tribes Were There in Premonarchic Israel?

If the tribes consisted of two or more *mishpahoth* organized geographically for defense purposes, the identity of tribes may have been fluid. We can imagine them as emerging, growing, shrinking, changing identity, reorganizing themselves to meet periodic threats as the need arose.[9]

The population of the highlands doubled by the end of the twelfth century. Estimates of the population of Israel at that time range from as low as

---

The belief that Israel consisted of twelve tribes descended from the twelve sons of one man is obviously folklore.

40,000 to as high as 120,000. If tribes were fluid, no one can venture a guess as to how many tribes there were before the coming of the monarchy. Historically, the number twelve had no significance at that time.

The Number Twelve

As we indicated above in our discussion of the J document, we are led to believe that during the reign of David, he, or his advisors, defined the boundaries of Israel and took a census to assist in the definition and governance of his territory. The purpose of the census was for taxation, military conscription, and corvée labor assessments. This twelve-part division had to enjoy some success from the monarchical viewpoint. The wealth of Jerusalem grew modestly under David, and the urban economy flourished magnificently under Solomon.[10] The author of the Deuteronomistic history presents the reader/listener with this specific understanding:

> Solomon had twelve officials over all Israel, who provided food for the king and his household; each one had to make provision for one month in the year. (1 Kgs 4:7)

Following this statement, the geographic areas assigned to the twelve officials are identified. Only five of these twelve Solomonic areas have names of the traditional twelve tribes: Ephraim, Manasseh, Issachar, Benjamin, and Judah. This report of the administrative districts has the effect of suggesting to us that the use of the number twelve had a relationship to the fact that there are twelve months in the year and that during the united monarchy there were twelve administrative districts.[11]

A problem is raised based on the fact that there is no one authoritative list of the twelve tribes in the Hebrew bible. There are conflicting lists. For example, in Deuteronomy 33 it is reported that Moses blessed each of the

---

There is no one authoritative list of the twelve tribes in the Hebrew bible.

---

tribes of Israel at the time of his death. Simeon does not appear and does not receive a blessing. Another interesting fact concerning Simeon is the location of the tribe. In DH (the Deuteronomistic history) the Prophet Ahijah announces to Jeroboam that the LORD will preserve one tribe for the house of David. The one tribe preserved for David was Judah. Simeon, geographically, was located south of Judah and obviously did not become part of the northern kingdom of Israel. Also, after the northern tribes secede, Solomon's son, Rehoboam, assembles 180,000 troops from the tribes of Judah and Benjamin. No mention is made of Simeon.[12]

Speaking of the southern area of Israel, it is interesting to note that it is probable that several groups, including Kenites and Calebites, both mentioned in Judges 1, almost made it to the tribal list. But their inclusion would have disturbed the necessity of maintaining the number twelve.

Frequently, arithmetic accuracy does not seem to be of importance when the twelve tribes are referred to.[13] The prophet Ahijah gives ten pieces of his garment to Jeroboam and is left with two pieces, even though he explicitly states that only one tribe will remain with the house of David. In the first census of Israel, reported in the book of Numbers (chapter 1), thirteen tribes are mentioned even if we eliminate Joseph.[14]

The division of Israel into twelve areas by David or Solomon became obsolete when the northern tribes seceded. The twelve-part administrative division lasted for almost a century.

Later Liturgical Significance of the Twelve Tribes

According to our reasoning, the significance of the twelve tribes related to the administrative divisions of David and Solomon would have had little practical value following secession of the northern tribes.

In Judah the twelve-tribe tradition would live on, at least in court literature. Centuries later, during the reign of Josiah, it is possible that a Jerusalem Levitical priesthood, with roots in the north, envisioning the restoration of the

The belief that there were twelve original tribes was revived and crystallized by the Josianic edition of the Deuteronomistic history.[15]

kingdom of David in the wake of the fatal decline of Assyria, recognized both the liturgical value of the twelve-part division of Israel and the contribution of this now ancient tradition of cohesive unity to preparing the people of Judah for the campaign to restore the northern territories. So the Deuteronomic circle embedded the twelve-tribe concept firmly into a reconstruction of the age of conquest, incorporating it in the Deuteronomistic history beginning with the scroll of Joshua. The twelve-tribe concept was also folded into the preface to the history, an early version of the book of Deuteronomy. There are liturgical overtones in Joshua where twelve stones are used to mark the place where the tribes of Israel crossed the Jordan River.

> The Israelites did as Joshua commanded. They took twelve stones out of the middle of the Jordan, according to the number of the tribes of the Israelites as the LORD told Joshua, carried them over with them to the place where they camped and laid them down there. (Jos 4:8)

Liturgical overtones continue when the twelve tribes later divide themselves between Mount Gerazim and Mount Ebal for the reading of the blessings and curses (Jos 8). These twelve tribes are named in Deuteronomy 27.

> When you have crossed over the Jordan these shall stand on Mount Gerazim for the blessing of the people: Simeon, Levi, Judah, Issachar, Joseph, and Benjamin. And these shall stand on Mount Ebal for the curse: Reuben, Gad, Ashur, Zebulon, Dan, and Naphtali. (Dt 27:11–13)[16]

Whatever its origin, the concept of Israel as the twelve tribes of Jacob was incorporated into the Josianic edition of the Deuteronomistic history as a contribution to the unification of the people of Judah to prepare them for the annexation of the northern provinces to restore the area of David's kingdom.

With the untimely death of Josiah (609) and the subjection of Judah—first as a vassal of Egypt, followed by the takeover of Judah by the Neo-Babylonians—the vision of the Deuteronomic circle temporarily dissolved into confusion and despair. But the seeds of the concept had been firmly planted. The concept endured in captivity, both in Babylon and Egypt, to become an entrenched belief of the scattered Judahite community.

We have a clue revealing the role that the concept of the twelve tribes played in postexilic Jerusalem. When the book of Exodus reached its canonical form, it included the following information. The elaborate breastplate of the high priest of the Jerusalem temple (the second temple), worn by the descendant of Aaron, would contain twelve stones.

> There shall be twelve stones with names corresponding to the names of the twelve sons of Israel. (Ex 28:21)

Postexilic Judahites returning from Babylon late in the sixth century under the leadership of the Aaronid priesthood considered themselves to be the only pure descendants of ancient Israel, in contrast to other Judahites located in various places, including a portion of the population of Judah that had not been carried into Babylonian captivity. If a setting similar to this existed—and we have reason to believe that it did—we would have an example of manufactured unity in the midst of actual diversity.

NOTES

1. A recent book, *The Book of J*, written by Harold Bloom, based on a translation by David Rosenberg (New York: Grove Weidenfeld, 1990), states that J was a woman. In keeping with tradition, we will use male pronouns in referring to J.

2. Robert and Mary Coote, *Power, Politics, and the Making of the Bible* (Minneapolis: Fortress Press, 1990), p. 29.

3. Coote, p. 28.

4. See chapter 49 of Genesis. This list of twelve tribes is identical to the list that appears in Joshua 7.

5. Read Joshua 7:14 and 1 Samuel 10:20–21. The NRSV translates the Hebrew word(s) *mishpahah, mishpahoth,* "clan" and "clans." Neighboring families within a clan may indeed have been related as a result of ongoing marriages between the members of the geographically close households.

6. David Hopkins, *The Highlands of Canaan*, chapter 9, "Risk Spreading and Labor Optimization."

7. Read section 298 entitled "Cross-Cutting Associations: The Exogamous Clan," pp. 298–301 in *Tribes of Yahweh*. My quotation is from p. 301.

8. P. 315 of *Tribes of Yahweh* and passim.

9. Rainer Albertz writes, in *A History of Israelite Religion* (p. 73), "...the tribal alliance of Israel is largely fictitious" and "...the clans could sometimes count themselves as being in one tribe and sometimes being in another."

10. See chapter 5, "Solomon's Tyranny," in Robert B. Coote's book *In Defense of Revolution: The Elohist History*, for a discussion of Jerusalem's prosperity during Solomon's reign.

11. Norman Gottwald writes in *Tribes*, "We can now assert that the historical origin of the twelve-tribe scheme...actually belonged to the period of the united monarchy" (p. 362).

12. Scholars who picture the twelve-tribe system as a reality during the

premonarchic period state that Simeon had ceased to exist by the time of the united monarchy.

13. In the first chapter of Judges, ten tribes are mentioned. Even though it is widely understood that the two sons of Joseph, Manasseh and Ephraim, each had his own tribal territory, instead of Joseph having one tribal allotment, in Judges 1 the tribe of Joseph is mentioned in addition to Ephraim and Manasseh. Later in the book of Judges, in the story of Deborah (Jgs 4 and 5), ten tribes are mentioned, six that responded to Deborah's call and four that did not respond. However, two of the tribes do not have traditional names. These two tribes are Gilead and Machir. Many scholars assume that Gilead is to be identified with Gad and Machir with Manasseh. There is no mention of Levi, Simeon, or Judah in the Deborah story.

14. The thirteen tribes are Reuben, Simeon, Gad, Judah, Issachar, Zebulun, Ephraim, Manasseh, Benjamin, Dan, Asher, Naphtali, Levi.

15. The stories of twelve tribes appeared in the J document, produced during the period of the united monarchy. We do not know anything about the popularity and/or the circulation of the J document in Judah after the secession of the northern tribes. During the exile and following the exile the J document was used as a major source in producing the Tetrateuch.

16. These tribes are the same tribes named in Genesis 49, where Jacob calls his sons to foretell their future. In Numbers 1, Joseph is replaced by Ephraim and Manasseh, and Levi is eliminated. In Deuteronomy 33, Levi appears, but Simeon is dropped. Deuteronomy 33 was a postexilic addition to the book of Deuteronomy.

6

Religious Practices of Early Israel

It is not possible to look in the bible for details concerning the religion of early Israel except in a very general way. The reason for this is that the picture of proto-Israel presented to us in the canonical Hebrew bible is an idealization of an ancient age, long past by the time of the history's composition. On the other hand, the Hebrew bible is our best source of informational detail concerning the religious practices of early Israel if we read between the lines and do not overinterpret the biblical record.

First, notice that the title of this chapter is not "The Religion of Early Israel." To speak of religion in the singular would not be accurate. There was no *uniformity* in religion such as that presented in the book of Joshua. In premonarchic Israel there was a variety of forms of Baalism. Later, when Yahweh became a god of Israel, different understandings of Yahweh produced different forms of Yahwism. There was no central authority for orthodoxy, no committee of priests or theologians to decide which theology was correct and which was heretical. There was no institution of religious education for prophets or religious leaders. Practices varied from location to location. On one level religious practices were determined by family tradition. On this level no external authority was recognized for guidance.

There are some scholars who believe that some of the activities attributed to Abraham, Isaac, and Jacob of the patriarchal period (described in Gn 12–35) were typical of the two-hundred-year period preceding the monarchy. This would include the building of altars at specific locations to mark special occasions (Noah, Abram, Isaac, and Jacob built altars) and the frequently referred-to practice of standing a stone on its end like a pillar and pouring olive oil on the stone.[1] The Hebrew word for this standing stone is *massebah.* In addition to the pillar, there was also a wooden pole.[2] Centuries later, during the reform of the late Judean monarch Josiah, Israel would be instructed to demolish altars and destroy the pillars.

Break down their altars, smash their pillars, burn their sacred poles. (Dt 12:3, read by Josiah from the book of the law as part of his reform)

On another level religion was regional. Family *(beth-av)* practices would differ from larger-social-group practices *(mishpahah)* just as family needs would differ from larger-group needs. A family would be concerned, along with agricultural fertility (crops and farm animals), with the birth of children, health, prosperity, marriage, and death, whereas a clan group would be concerned with both territorial fertility and protection from hostile forces or enemies. As we have said, families related to each other in regional alliances similar to clans *(mishpahoth)*.

SOME ALTARS AT SHRINES IN PRESTATE ISRAEL

CHART 3

During the period before the monarchy, altars were erected at many regional holy places. Later, sometimes centuries later, the altars were historized and attributed to a patriarch or ancient hero of Israel who was seen as a champion of Yahweh.

Location	Attributed to	Scripture Reference
Hebron	Abraham	Gn 13:18
Beersheba	Isaac	Gn 26:25
Bethel	Jacob	Gn 35:1
Rephidim	Moses	Ex 17:15
Mount Ebal	Joshua	Jos 8:30
Ophrah	Gideon	Jgs 6:24
Ramah	Samuel	1 Sm 7:17

Wherever there was a shrine there may have been some kind of recognized regional authority, perhaps a holy person or an emerging priesthood. While the recognized need for synchronization was still centuries in Israel's future, there may have been connections and communication between shrines that were geographically related.

Practices varied in detail and perspective at Shechem, Shiloh, Bethel, Hebron, Beersheba, Megiddo, Gilgal, and wherever a shrine was established. There was the possibility that although there was no one central authoritative location, a number of locations, or shrines, could have been linked together in some cooperative way. The holy person Samuel (identified as a seer, a prophet, a judge, and a priest[3]) is said to be responsible for a circuit including Bethel, Gilgal, Mizpah, and Ramah (1 Sm 7:15–17).

So a number of assumptions about community understandings are possible. These assumptions are based on Canaanite practices, some of which would be condemned (centuries later) in the Hebrew scrolls as practices not suitable for Israel, not pleasing to Yahweh, an abomination to Yahweh, and so forth.

Ten Assumptions Concerning Prestate Religion in Israel

Here are the ten assumptions: (1) The religion of early Israel was rural in character.[4] (2) It was tied to agriculture and the changing seasons. (3) The practices of the earliest Israelites were identical to the practices of the inhabitants of the surrounding area of Palestine and Syria. (4) Religious practices of early Israel were related to a Canaanite form of Baalism and were concerned with fertility. (5) The fragmentation and fractured topography of the land tended to spawn dozens of varieties of Baalism, differing in content, practice, and understanding from family to family, from village to village, from area to area. (6) Behind the religion of early Israel was an elaborate Ugaritic (northern Canaanite) mythology that the authors and editors of the Hebrew bible have masterfully hidden,

---

YAHWISM IN PRESTATE ISRAEL

CHART 4

1. Yahweh was first known in the rough, precultivated wilderness environment south of Israel.

2. Yahweh was introduced in Israel by a group that had had a significant exodus experience.

3. Yahweh was a warrior god.

4. As a god of liberation, Yahweh's earlier impact was not on religious practices of families but on larger segments of society.

5. An ancient tradition identifies a wooden chest as a Yahwist cult item.

6. Yahweh as a god of prestate Israel did not replace El, Baal, or Asherah.

ignored, and weeded out.[5] (7) There were two levels of religious practices: family activities and community practices. (8) The worship of Yahweh as a warrior god who would fight for his people, the humbler classes of society, was introduced to northern Israel by one or several of the groups[6] that joined Israel, and the popularity of Yahweh worship spread in Israel because of its functionality. (9) Yahweh did not replace El, a high god of the Canaanites, but was worshiped along with El. There was no monotheism in early Israel. (10) Just as there was no one version of Baalism, there also was no one version of Yahwism.

The Three Annual Festivals

It is possible that the rural culture of Canaan held three areawide agricultural festivals a year. In early Israel these three festivals were not historized (with exodus and wilderness traditions), observance was not centralized,[7] and the festivals were not related to Yahweh.[8] As time went on, of course, these three festivals became transformed into Israelite festivals and became tied to unique Israelite Yahwistic traditions.[9] The Israelite forms of the three festivals are described in the Hebrew bible many times (Ex 23,[10] Ex 34, Lv 23, Nm 28, Dt 16). By the time these written descriptions of the three festivals appeared, the purely Canaanite origins had been obscured.

The three festivals were these. The festival of unleavened bread marked the beginning of the barley season and was observed for seven days in the spring (March–April). The festival of harvest (feast of weeks) marked the end of the grain harvest in June. The feast of ingathering (feast of huts, or booths) was tied to the grape and olive harvest in September at the end of the year.[11]

As was common in the ancient Near East, animal sacrifice was part of both community festival and family practice. Other than to acknowledge that there was a widespread belief that animal sacrifice was pleasing to the gods, it is safe to assume that there may have been a great variety of understandings of the meaning and purpose of sacrifices, differing from group to group. Centuries later in Judah, the creation of scrolls such as Leviticus would attempt to explain extensively the how and the why of sacrificial procedures. We will comment later on these greatly complicated procedures and their attempt to explain the meaning of sacrifice. It is interesting to note that references to acts of animal sacrifice in the prestate period are very uncomplicated and straightforward with no attempt to explain procedure or meaning.

Superstition and Folk Religion

The above discussion concerning more or less *public* community activities and beliefs existed parallel to a plethora of superstitious beliefs widespread in the rural areas of prescientific times. Robert Coote writes in *Early Israel:*

An entire cast of village gods and goddesses, spirits, sprites, demons, goblins, and genies were thought to participate in the process of production and reproduction....Magic was real, the evil eye a peril. The dead remained part of the community....odd persons offered services to be used and feared.[12]

The scriptures provide us with glimpses of these practices. Saul is reported to have spoken with Samuel after his death by obtaining the services of a medium (1 Sm 28:3–25). It is profitable to read carefully the story of Saul's encounter with the medium of Endor. In the tradition as preserved by the historian, there is no skepticism concerning the medium's power to recall the deceased Samuel from beyond the grave. At one point the medium refers to Saul's previous action—

...how he [Saul] has cut off the mediums and wizards from the land. (1 Sm 28:8)

In this story, just as in laws forbidding mediums, wizards, soothsayers, and sorcerers, there are no words or expressions questioning the authenticity or reality of the skills being condemned. Even in monarchical Israel the so-called world of the occult was looked upon without doubt as a reality.

In the reforms of Josiah we read:

...Josiah put away the mediums, wizards, teraphim, idols, and all the abominations that were seen in the land of Judah and Jerusalem. (2 Kgs 23:24)

In Exodus 22:18 we read, "You shall not permit a female sorcerer [a witch] to live."

It is in conjunction with practices of this nature that child sacrifice is forbidden in Deuteronomy:

No one shall be found among you who makes a son or daughter pass through fire, or who practices divination, or is a soothsayer, or an augur, or a sorcerer, or one who casts spells, or who consults ghosts or spirits, or who seeks oracles from the dead. (18:10–11)

There were other dark practices of which we have only hints such as this prohibition in Leviticus 19:28.

You shall not make any gashes in your flesh for the dead.

Summary

Although we have no primary sources for a reconstruction of religion in premonarchic Israel, there are some broad statements that can be safely made. But caution is needed. It is safer to say too little about these matters than too much. The approach to history found in the bible has been described as the great-men-make-history approach. While we should avoid understanding a period of the past in terms of one or several significant persons, it is true that the reported activity of ancient heroes can supply valid clues to past activity of a society. In summarizing the religion of prestate Israel, however, we should not be overinfluenced by the theology of scrolls produced centuries after the fact. With these things in mind, we make the following suggestions:

(1) The first god of Israel was El and the earliest form of religion consisted of rural varieties of Canaanite Baalism. An ancient mythology provided a background, but little evidence of this mythology has survived in the Hebrew bible.[13]

(2) Yahweh, a warrior god from the wilderness south of Judah, was introduced to Israel (the northern clans) by a group that had had an important exodus experience. Yahwism spread, but the fragmented geography of Israel produced various forms of both Yahwism and Baalism.

(3) There were several levels of religious experience involving the extended family and the community (areawide agricultural feasts, for example). In addition there was much private superstitious activity typical of prescientific rural life.

(4) Throughout Israel there were many examples of theological contradiction and inconsistency, but there was no one in a position to take notice or be concerned.

(5) Priesthoods associated with regional shrines began to emerge, and efforts were made to control ritual and belief in certain areas (Shechem, Gibeon,[14] Hebron, Shiloh[15]).

(6) Since there was no state, there was no state religion.[16]

NOTES

1. For example, tradition has Jacob erecting a pillar at Bethel and pouring oil on it (Gn 35:14).

2. The pillar has been seen as a phallic symbol. The pole may have been a carved wooden image of the goddess Asherah. The Hebrew word is *asherim*, the male plural form of the singular feminine Asherah. A. D. H. Mayes writes in *Deuteronomy*, p. 184, "[It] was a man-made object of wood, which could be cut down and burned…it is probable that it was a carved wooden image of the goddess rather than simply an upright wooden pole."

3. Samuel is not explicitly called a priest, but he lives in a temple at Shiloh with a priest, and he is authorized to offer animal sacrifices on special occasions.

4. In part II of this book, we will discuss the emergence of urban religion and the place of urban religion in Israel, beginning with the establishment of Jerusalem as a national capital by the house of David.

5. There are several things that can be said here. First of all, there was no attempt by the authors of the Hebrew bible to re-create the days of early *historical* Israel. If this would have been a possible goal of the historian (and it was not), then there would have been some references to the mythology. (2) This mythology was largely unknown to bible scholars until 1929, when Ras Shamra was excavated (Ugarit), a city on the northwest seacoast of Syria. Consult the *New Jerome Biblical Commentary*, pp. 215–16.

6. The group that introduced Yahweh as a warrior god to Israel is sometimes called the exodus group, or the Moses group. This group, after escaping from enslavement in Egypt, spent a period of time in the wilderness south of Judah. The wilderness experience (a positive experience) became an important part of Israel tradition and is first referred to in the books of Amos, Hosea, and Jeremiah. The wilderness experience in the Tetrateuch (the first four books of the bible) is a later literary production of which we will have more to say later.

7. Brevard Childs, in discussing the work of a scholar who stated that the description of the observance of the three festivals in Exodus 23 was centralized, states that this point remains highly debatable. See *The Book of Exodus* (Philadelphia: Westminster, 1974), p. 484. Some scholars locate the observance of the three festivals within the *mishpahoth*, the regional alliances of families. For example, see De Geus, *The Tribes of Israel* (1976), p. 143.

8. We do not know when Yahweh, a warrior god, gained control of atmospheric phenomena. Perhaps this was understood early as necessary to insure martial victories and deliverance from enemies.

9. Much later in Israel, the three agricultural feasts were historized. The first festival, unleavened bread, was joined with passover and was understood to commemorate the tradition of the night that Israel fled from Egypt. The second festival, weeks, observed seven weeks after unleavened bread, would become part of instructions reported to have come directly from Yahweh to Moses. The third feast, booths or huts, would later become a reminder of the wilderness-journey tradition when Israel dwelt in booths (Lv 23:43).

10. The earliest description of the three annual festivals is found in Exodus 23: 14–17. This description appears in the collection of laws traditionally called the Book of the Covenant. This title, from my viewpoint, is unfortunately misleading. It is taken from a sentence that appears in Exodus 24:7 and is not directly tied to the collection in Exodus 21–23. Hans Boecker

(among other scholars) refers to the collection as the "so-called Book of the Covenant."

11. While our chief sources for the religious practices of early Israel are practices condemned in the scriptures, not all practices condemned in scrolls produced later can be attributed to early Israel. Here are some examples: (1) The use of solar imagery as referred to in Josiah's reform activity—

He (Josiah) removed the horses that the kings of Judah had dedicated to the sun...then he burned the chariots of the sun with fire. (2 Kgs 23:11)

—became part of worship in Judah during the monarchic period. (2) An Assyrian form of worshiping the host of heaven was introduced in Judah (from Assyria) during the monarchy. We are told that Josiah deposed the idolatrous priests who made offerings in the high places at the cities of Judah and around Jerusalem:

...who made offerings...to the sun, the moon, the constellations, and all the host of heaven. (2 Kgs 23:5)

(3) While some aspects of Assyrian solar worship may have influenced Jerusalem temple practice, sun worship was widespread in the ancient Near East, and sun worship of some form was probably included in premonarchic Israel. We don't have any examples to cite, however. Consult the article by Karel van der Toorn on sun worship in the *Anchor Bible Dictionary* (New York: Doubleday, 1992), pp. VI: 237–39.

12. Robert Coote, *Early Israel*, p. 26.

13. Of course, the only accounts we have of life in proto-Israel are found in Joshua and Judges, scrolls written centuries after the fact by conscientious scribes with a strong theological and social agenda. Since they wrote in the late seventh century, we do not know how much of the ancient Canaanite mythology was known to these scribes or if they were informed at all.

14. The function of Gibeon as a recognized principal high place lasted into the monarchy. Tradition tells us that seven sons of the house of Saul were put to death there (2 Sm 21:6–9), and Solomon is said to have offered many sacrifices there (1 Kgs 3:4).

15. In 1 Samuel we learn that there was a temple at Shiloh administered by the priests of the house of Eli.

16. In this chapter we have not commented on the *chest of Yahweh*, later called by many names, the most popular of which was the *ark of the covenant*. A most interesting ironic story is told in 1 Samuel 4–6. We will comment on the moving of the chest of Yahweh to Jerusalem by David in part II.

Part II
DAVID AND SOLOMON
(1000–922 B.C.E.)

7

The Rise of David

It is unfortunate that the only source of detailed information we have concerning David is in the Hebrew bible. No mention of David is found in the literature of the ancient Near East.[1]

For this reason it is necessary, as we read and study the portion of the scrolls that record the history of David (from 1 Sm 16 to 1 Kgs 2 inclusive), that we keep in mind that there are at least three levels of authorship for these chapters. (a) There are primary sources, copies of ancient written material possibly dating from the time of the reported events or shortly thereafter. If this material existed, we have to assume that David had at his service a cadre of scribes and that he recognized the value of written materials to bolster, support, and strengthen his establishment of a dynasty.[2] (b) These Davidic writings are only available to us interwoven with the theological writings of a Josianic historian who produced the earliest version of the Deuteronomistic history (DH), four hundred years after the death of David. (c) There are also the words of an editor or redactor who wrote during the period of the exile, following the destruction of Jerusalem, the temple, and the scattering of the people of Judah (after 597 B.C.E.).

In all there are forty-two chapters of narrative dealing with David. This is significant because there is no other person in the Deuteronomistic history (Joshua, Judges, Samuel, Kings) who even comes close to this coverage.[3] We must acknowledge that the historic person behind this immense body of narrative history, folklore, and theological discourse must have been an extraordinary person of tremendous influence.

Since we have mentioned three categories of literature in the above paragraph—narrative history, folklore, and theology—let us give an example of each. The anointing of David by Samuel the prophet *(nabi),* the incident that begins the Davidic material, is pure theology. In the theology of the Josianic historian, it was the most natural thing in the world to believe that the first two kings of Israel would have been anointed by a prophet. Both of these anointings

51

were performed in secret, Saul in 1 Samuel 10:1 and David in 1 Samuel 16. The theological implication is that Yahweh was the selector of these kings, the shaper of history, and that his messengers were the first to inform the kings of their selection. But the reader is not prepared for the act of anointing a king in advance by a prophet. Notice that the historian reports the event as if it were the most natural thing in the world. And the persons receiving the anointing (Saul and David) seem to know exactly what is happening and the meaning of the ceremony. The historian shows his theological hand; for him, in the seventh century during the reign of Josiah, this was an ancient tradition. In reality the anointing of David by Samuel was not history. It was theology.

A classic example of folklore is the polished story of the Philistine giant, Goliath of Gath. A reading of the complete story (1 Sm 17) makes this obvious. It is interesting to note that in a later historical account of David's dwelling in Gath in a successful effort to shake off Saul's constant pursuit (1 Sm 27), no mention is made of Goliath the giant.[4]

An example of history would be the settlement of his private army in territory controlled by Philistines and his communication and cooperation with Philistines (King Achish of Gath, for example) during the period when he was eluding Saul while building his own following as a chief of Judah.

The Rise of David: An Independent Scroll

The cluster of incidents that tell the story of David's rise during the reign of Saul is found in a section bracketed by two anointings, 1 Samuel 16 and 2 Samuel 5:5. The first anointing is by Samuel in Bethlehem (1 Sm 16) and the last anointing is in Hebron by the elders of Israel as king of all Israel (2 Sm 5).[5] The two anointings were not part of the original scroll, a scroll produced by scribes of David's scriptorium.[6] This scroll had two main goals: (1) to present a noble picture of David as a completely supportive, loyal, and devoted servant of Saul and the house of Saul; and (2) to indicate that David was the perfect servant of Yahweh—Yahweh, who had rejected Saul as king and had chosen David, continually providing David with protection, guidance, and blessing.

The two anointings that now bracket "the Rise of David" were added by the Josianic historian when the independent scroll was incorporated in the Deuteronomic history. So the primary purpose of the scroll had been to promote the legitimacy of David's reign during his lifetime and to improve public relations (an area where David was skilled) by changing the skeptical attitudes of groups within Israel that harbored doubts about the wisdom of supporting David, a Judean, as king for the northern territories. David had to overcome a reputation among some northern clans as an outsider, an outlaw, and an enemy.

In the last few decades scholars, using sociological and political theory, have tended to present David as a shrewd, ambitious Judean sheikh, who did what was necessary to achieve his political ends, including consorting with the Philistine enemies of Israel.[7] In the area south of Israel, David became a vassal of the Philistines and was assigned the city of Ziklag as his base.

ORGANIZATION OF WRITINGS CONCERNING DAVID **CHART 5**	
The Rise of David Begins with anointing by Samuel and ends with David as king of both Judah and Israel	1 Sm 16– 2 Sm 5:5
The Apex of David's Reign Capture of Jerusalem, relocating the chest of Yahweh, and the unconditional covenant of Nathan's announcement	2 Sm 5:6– 2 Sm 7
David's Wars and Additional Material David's victories over Moabites, Ammonites, and hired Arameans	2 Sm 8–10
The Decline of David (Court History) Begins with the sin with Bathsheba and ends with David's death	2 Sm 11–20; 1 Kgs 1–2
Four chapters are not included in the above chart: 2 Sm 21–24.	

During this period David was the commander of a small private mercenary army of from four hundred to six hundred men, a practice that David continued throughout his reign as king of Jerusalem.[8]

The scroll we have called "the Rise of David" tells the captivating story of a young warrior from Bethlehem who intensely wanted to serve and support Saul and who loved the house of Saul. David loved the crown prince, Jonathan, and married Michal, a daughter of Saul. But David's good intentions were defeated at every turn by Saul's intense jealousy, a defect of psychotic proportions that finally contributed to the rejection of Saul by Yahweh.

So at the core of this section we have a cluster of incidents relating the young David's interactions with Saul and the house of Saul. Its origin dates to the reign of David. David understood the value of public relations and the role of written documents in changing opinion. One of the benefits for modern students is the picture of Saul that emerges. Although Saul was not a monarch typical of the ancient Near East, it is obvious that he was a powerful chief with a large following and a key transitory figure in the emergence of the monarchy in Israel.[9]

Because of Saul's widespread support, which David must have coveted, the incidents in the cluster were carefully composed to soften the opposition and feelings of ill will harbored by former supporters of Saul toward David. Numerous activities of David and his band were justified and cast in a good light, making David appear as an obedient and loyal subject of Saul, forced to flee Saul's presence because of an evil spirit that came on Saul, causing Saul to misinterpret David's good intentions.

> …an evil spirit from God rushed upon Saul, and he raved within his house, while David was playing the lyre, as he did day by day. Saul had his spear in his hand: and Saul threw the spear, for he thought, "I will pin David to the wall." But David eluded him twice. (1 Sm 18:10)

Further, we read that in David's efforts to acquire Saul's daughter Michal as his wife, Saul planned to make David fall into the hands of the Philistines (1 Sm 18:25). Both Michal and Jonathan intervene to save David from their father's murderous intentions.

When David flees to southern wilderness areas, Saul and his army pursue David. Several times David is reported to have had opportunity to kill Saul, but he refuses. He says to Abishai:

> …who can raise his hand against the LORD's anointed and be guiltless?…As the LORD lives, the LORD will strike him down; or his day will come to die; or he will go down into battle and perish. (1 Sm 26:9–10)

It is interesting to remember that when David calls Saul the LORD's anointed, David is also the LORD's anointed according to the canonical scriptures (1 Sm 16).

When David and his entourage of six hundred men finally settle in the area of Gath and are granted the city of Ziklag by Achish, king of Gath, we are told that Saul no longer sought him (1 Sm 27:4).

Finally, when Saul and Jonathan are slain in the famous battle against the Philistines on Mount Gilboa, David and his band mourned greatly:

> They mourned and wept, and fasted until evening for Saul and his son Jonathan, and for the army of the LORD and for the house of Israel, because they had fallen by the sword. (2 Sm 1:12)

Within several years both Abner, Saul's general and power behind the throne, and Ishbaal, Saul's son and successor, were murdered, and David became king of both Judah and the federation of northern clans. With the acceptance of David as king of all Israel, the document known as "the Rise of David," produced by David's scribes early in his reign, to justify David's activities in the wilderness of Judah during the reign of Saul, came to an end.[10]

"The Rise of David" had two purposes, however. Not only are the activities of David justified, blamed on the unreasonable persecution by a troubled Saul, defeating David's desire to be a loyal and faithful subject, but there is a second theme concerning David's relationship with Yahweh.[11]

David and Yahweh

Repeatedly, in the independent literary tradition we are examining, the guidance and protection of Yahweh are tied to David's decisions. Here are five examples:

(1) When David faces Goliath he states, "The battle is Yahweh's and he will give you into our hand" (1 Sm 17:47).

(2) When Saul tries to kill David, we are told "Saul was afraid of David because Yahweh (the LORD) was with him" (1 Sm 18:12).

(3) When Jonathan warned David in the wilderness of Saul's plans, the two of them made a covenant "before Yahweh" (1 Sm 23:18).

(4) In David's encounter with Abigail, David says, "Blessed be Yahweh, the God of Israel, who sent you to meet me today" (1 Sm 25:32).

(5) Before David avenged the destruction of Ziklag, his city before Hebron, David enquired of Yahweh (1 Sm 30:8).

In the conclusion of part I of this book, we stated that the first god of Israel was El, a high god of the Canaanite pantheon. Yahweh was introduced to the northern clans (Israel) by a group that joined Israel, a group with an exodus experience. In addition to El and Yahweh, Baal and Asherah were gods in prestate Israel. There may have been others.

Was it possible that David was historically an advocate for Yahweh and that, with the accession of David, a southern, wilderness form of Yahwism became the official religion of Israel's new capital, Jerusalem?

There are reasons for caution in reaching this conclusion. For example,

(1) the Deuteronomistic history that contains "the Rise of David" was compiled almost four hundred years after the fact; (2) it was compiled by a circle
that championed Yahweh and Yahweh only.

Hear O Israel; The LORD [YHWH] is our God, the LORD alone.
(Dt 6:4)

Although primary sources were used and scrolls of independent authorship
were incorporated into the Deuteronomic history, such as the Elijah cycle and
the succession narrative,[12] we do not have these primary sources and do not
know how these sources were shaped and edited.

On the plus side, however, supporting the view that David was indeed a
champion of Yahweh to the exclusion of other gods, there are other traditions
to be considered (see chapter 8). Also, if the J document was produced by
scribes of the scriptorium of David, then there would be little doubt that David
was a promoter of Yahwism. Some recent scholars have raised serious doubts
concerning the date and circumstances of J's origin.[13] Some have even challenged the very existence of J as a separate scroll.

But the form of Yahwism that David would have brought to Jerusalem
may have differed from the forms already present in the area of the northern
clans, Ephraim and Benjamin. The residents of the central hill country were
primarily subsistence farmers. Even Saul is pictured as plowing his field. All
David traditions, however, identify him as a warrior, leader of an outlaw band,
moving frequently from location to location in the wilderness of Judah, living
by his wits. He is never a settled, subsistence farmer. His perception of
Yahweh as a warrior god would have been closer to the roots of the origin of
primitive Yahweh worship.

In our next chapter we turn to two traditions associated with the reign of
David: the capture of Jerusalem and the moving of the chest of Yahweh to
Jerusalem.

NOTES

1. Two ancient references to the House of David have recently been discussed in subsequent issues of the *Biblical Archaeological Review*. The first
reference, in Aramaic, was found on a fragment of a stela, a victory monument
found at Dan (*BAR*, March/April 1994). The second is in Moabite script on the
black basalt Mesha stela telling of a ninth-century Moabite rebellion (*BAR*,
May/June 1994).

2. Robert and Mary Coote, in *Power, Politics, and the Making of the
Bible* (Minneapolis: Fortress, 1990), describe the output and purpose of
David's scriptorium in chapter 4, "David Begins the Bible."

3. After David's forty-two chapters of coverage, the whole history of Israel for over three centuries is covered in only forty-six chapters (1 Kgs 2–2 Kgs 25).

4. A doublet appears in 2 Samuel 21:19 naming Elhanan of Bethlehem as the slayer of Goliath.

5. At that time there may not have been a group representative of Israel called the elders of Israel. The report that this body came to Hebron with authority to speak and act for the northern clans is the work of the Josianic historian. It is a continuation of the idealized concept of Israel that the historian first put forth in the book of Joshua.

6. It is our suggestion that during the reign of David an independent scroll was produced by scribes in the employ of David defending, promoting, and justifying his actions in the southern wilderness (of Judah) during the reign of Saul. We have called this document "the Rise of David." Its purpose was to influence the attitudes of supporters of Saul, who opposed David and thought of him as a dangerous opportunist who was unworthy to be king of Israel.

The material found in this independent scroll is now located in 1 Samuel 16 to 2 Samuel 2, bracketed by two anointings that were added later, possibly by a Josianic historian. The historian updated the language and grammar of the scroll to make it readable in Josiah's time but did not make major changes in the content.

We date the production of the original scroll during the reign of David. It is an apologia, and there would have been no reason to generate it *after* the reign of David. By the time Solomon became king, opposition from supporters of Saul was a shadow of its former self.

The same scribes who wrote "the Rise of David" may also have produced the document now known as J. According to David Ord and Robert Coote, in *The Bible's First History* (Fortress, 1989), J, like "the Rise of David," was produced to shape attitudes and to influence those whose support David needed. See note 1 above.

7. See *The History of Ancient Palestine* by Gosta W. Ahlstrom, pp. 458–66; *A History of Israel* by H. Jagersma, pp. 95–99; and *Power, Politics and the Making of the Bible* by Robert and Mary Coote, pp. 25–28.

8. David's private army contained mercenaries including Cherethites and Pelethites. His private army may have captured the city of Jerusalem near the beginning of his reign, making Jerusalem his private possession. Late in David's reign the private army assisted Joab in the defeat of an uprising led by Shebna, a Benjaminite:

> Joab's men went out after him (Shena), along with the Cherethites, the Pelethites, and all the warriors. (2 Sm 20:7)

9. In Hebrew Saul is called a ruler (*nagid*) in Israel. In the stories of David, David is said to have recognized Saul as the King of Israel. Saul has been recognized as a judge, a peasant king, and a charismatic ruler. Judah was not part of the territory ruled by Saul.

10. It is frequently pointed out that David almost fought against Saul in the battle that ended his life. Only the protests of the Philistine military leaders to King Achish of Gath saved David from this involvement. So why include this story in the scroll called "the Rise of David"? There are several explanations. Perhaps the scribes got carried away with their goal of presenting David as a trusted loyal servant. The words of Achish to David sound like fiction to me.

Then Achish called David and said to him,

"As the LORD lives, you have been honest, and to me it seems right that you should march out and in with me in the campaign; for I have found nothing wrong in you from the day of your coming to me until today." (1 Sm 29:6)

Also, the story *proves* that David did not participate in the fatal battle against Saul and Jonathan.

11. There is a folkloristic form of narrative art produced to defend the successful usurpation of the throne, of which "the Rise of David" is a good example.

12. The succession narrative, or court history, may not have been included in the first edition of DH. This novella, by its very greatness, distracts rather than contributes to the primary goal of the circle that produced DH. Inclusion of the court history dilutes the thrust of the theological history. This may also have been true of the Elijah and Elisha cycles. See pp. 95–100 in the book by Steven McKenzie, *The Trouble with Kings*.

13. In 1977 R. Rendtorff challenged the existence of J as a continuing source in the Pentateuch, and J. Van Seters in 1986 argued that J was an exilic product of the Persian period.

8

David in Jerusalem and the Chest of Yahweh

Our task in the next several chapters is to examine a new, urban form of Israelite religion that first emerged when David took possession of the Jebusite fortress of Jerusalem in the early tenth century. The facts concerning David appearing in the Hebrew bible are layered with at least four centuries of tradition, along with narrative accounts that can only be described as theological. As students we must remember that the theology about David was unknown to the historical David.

The Capture of Jerusalem

The king and his men marched to Jerusalem against the Jebusites....David took the stronghold of Zion, which is now the city of David. (2 Sm 5:6–7)

References to Jerusalem in ancient Near Eastern writing date back to 2000 B.C.E. The so-called city-state was a fortress located on an important east-west road linking the two major trade routes—the Via Maris, along the coast of the Mediterranean, and the King's Highway, which ran north and south, east of the Jordan River.

Details concerning the capture of Jerusalem are brief and vague. The feat was accomplished by David's private army (David's men). We remember that David's family had its roots in Bethlehem, a satellite village of Jerusalem. As a youth David may have wandered freely in and around the vicinity of Jerusalem. Familiarity with the terrain may have contributed to the easy capture of the city.

Despite the crude reference to the proverbial belief that the blind and the lame could have defended Jerusalem,[1] the capture of the city was quick and clean. It is reported in Judges 1:21 that the Jebusites continued to live in Jerusalem "to this day." And it is later reported that David *purchased* the threshing floor of a prominent Jebusite, Araunah,[2] to erect an altar for Yahweh (2 Sm 25:18–25).

One of the difficulties faced by the modern student is the tendency to picture the city of Jerusalem before David as being much larger than it was. David's Jerusalem was nothing like the modern city or even the Jerusalem of New Testament times. It is even possible that the Josianic historian was influenced by the city of Jerusalem in Josiah's time when he wrote about David. Walled fortresses in premonarchic times located at strategic locations are sometimes referred to by scholars as city-states. This term is misleading. Jerusalem before David was very small, houses crowded together, the streets little more than alleys. David extended the city to the north, and the threshing floor of Araunah was further north, outside the new walls built by David. Solomon would extend the city still further north and enclose the threshing floor for the building of the temple.[3]

David had had experience administering a city at Ziklag and Hebron but may have valued the Jebusite administrative apparatus he inherited. It is to the implications for the religion of Israel resulting from the establishment of Jerusalem as the new capital—the royal city—that we direct our attention.

Moving the Chest of Yahweh to Jerusalem

The Josianic historian included in his narrative of David's establishment of Jerusalem a two-part, detailed story of the relocation of the chest (ark) of Yahweh from a location in the north to Jerusalem (2 Sm 6). This transfer of the chest to Jerusalem has been commonly cited by biblical scholars as an act of political shrewdness on the part of David, uniting a central religious symbol from Israel (the north) with both Judah and Jerusalem. Questions concerning the historicity of this event have recently been raised.[4]

In the Deuteronomistic history the story of David's moving of the chest of Yahweh to Jerusalem (2 Sm 6) is preceded by a narrative found in 1 Sm 4:1–7:2, traditionally called the ark narrative. The ark narrative is a strange, complicated story of a miraculous Israelite palladium captured by the Philistines in battle with Israel. The Philistines first take the ark to Ashdod, but the ark causes the Philistine god Dagon to fall on his face and lose his head and his hands. The people of Ashdod are terrified and stricken with tumors, so the ark is moved to Gath and then Ekron, where similar curses are experienced. (Ashdod, Gath, and Ekron were three of the five Philistine cities.) Finally the ark is returned to Israel.

But even in Israel the ark continues to carry a curse with it (1 Sm 6:19–7:2). Later, when David tries to move the ark, it erupts again.

When they came to the threshing floor of Nacon, Uzzah reached out his hand to the ark of God and took hold of it, for the oxen shook it. The anger of the LORD was kindled against Uzzah; and God struck him there because he reached out his hand to the ark….David was angry because the LORD had burst forth with an outburst upon Uzzah. (2 Sm 6:6–9)

The ark narrative is obviously an example of classic folklore. The Josianic historian artfully interfaces the folkloristic account of the ark with what the historian would like to present as an important moment in the history of Israel, the moving of the ark to Jerusalem by David. In our assessment of the historicity of facts concerning David, we have little doubt that David acquired the Jebusite city of Jerusalem as the neutral capital for the new monarchy. When it comes to the moving of the ark into Jerusalem, we have questions. It was our conclusion in part I of this book that prestate Israel had a plurality of Yahwistic cults. It is highly unlikely that the northern territory of Israel had a single, recognized ark symbol such as the one presented to us in DH.

The Legend of the Wandering Ark

In order to understand the ark, it is necessary for us to recognize that there are no less than three separate and distinct traditions (and maybe more) concerning the ark of the covenant. The oldest is preserved for us in the ark narrative (1 Sm). Later, during the reign of Josiah, the Deuteronomic circle would present a largely demythologized ark, a chest made of acacia wood for the purpose of holding the tablets of the law.

So I made an ark of acacia wood.…[I] came down from the mountain, and put the tablets in the ark that I had made; and they are there as the LORD commanded me. (Dt 10:3–5)

The third tradition is a priestly tradition. Here the ark is covered with gold, inside and out. The poles used to carry the ark are also covered with gold. Two large winged cherubs sit on a special lid called the mercy seat, their wings touching each other (Ex 25:10–22).

The historian used many ancient sources in putting together the Josianic edition of the Deuteronomistic history (DH). Why he chose the sources he used and how he used them are subjects worthy of further study. But the picture of the chest as presented in the ark narrative may have been a harmonization of local traditions concerning a number of cultic items serving similar purposes. As we see it, there were two main functions for these cultic items.

**THREE DIVERSE TRADITIONS
CONCERNING THE CHEST OF YAHWEH**

(Called by many names, including *ark of the covenant*)

CHART 6

TRADITION	SOURCE	SCRIPTURE
A mystical palladium	Prestate Israel	1 Sm 4:1–7:2; 2 Sm 6:1–17
A plain wooden chest of acacia wood to hold the tablets of the law (Demythologized)	Descendants of Levitical priests of Shechem	Dt 10:1–5
Gold-covered cultic object with a gold lid and two winged cherubs	Aaronid priesthood (exilic)	Ex 25:10–22; 1 Kgs 8:3–8

Some Names for the Chest of Yahweh:

ark of God	(1 Sm 4)
ark of YAHWEH (the LORD)	"
ark of the covenant	"
ark of the testimony	(Nm 4:5)
ark of the God of Israel	(7 times)

Measurements: Chest: 2 1/2 x 1 1/2 x 1 1/2 cubits
                 Wing of a cherub: 5 cubits
                 Height of a cherub: 10 cubits

(a) The first was to signify the actual presence of God. Where the symbol was, there was God. Or specifically, in the canonical scriptures, where the ark was, there was Yahweh. In the ark narrative, for example, when the Philistines learn that the ark has come into the camp of the Israelites, they are reported to have said,

> Gods have come into the camp....These are the gods who struck the Egyptians with every sort of plague in the wilderness. (1 Sm 4:5–8)

(b) The second function of the central religious symbol was to make it possible for an individual or group to determine the god's will. An example is found in a rare reference to the ark in the book of Judges.

> And the Israelites *inquired of the LORD* (for the ark of the covenant was there in those days…), saying, "Shall we go out once more to do battle against our kinsfolk the Benjaminites, or shall we desist?" (Jgs 20:27–28)

The ark narrative had accrued multiple layers by the time the historian incorporated it into DH.[5]

In accordance with our conclusion in part I of this book, we are suggesting that the beginning of political unity under the leadership of Saul was not accompanied by a religious unity between the families and clans of Israel to the extent that there was one central cultic object for all the tribes, such as the chest of Yahweh. It is more likely that there was a plurality of so-called central cult objects fulfilling the functions mentioned above, (a) assuring the presence of Yahweh and (b) providing a place of divination.[6]

The plurality of local cultic objects was replaced in the Deuteronomistic history by the legend of the wandering ark. To bolster the fiction of Israel's unity, the historian pictured one ark for all the tribes, an ark carried by the Levitical priests when Israel entered the land (Jos 3) and moved from location to location as time passed. Following the lead of the Deuteronomic historian, the Aaronid priestly circle picked up on the legend of the wandering ark and projected it further back into Israel's past. In this form it is currently found in three books of the Tetrateuch, Exodus, Leviticus, Numbers.

LOCATIONS OF THE CHEST OF YAHWEH

The Theory of the Wandering Ark in the Deuteronomistic History

CHART 7

Shittim	Jos 3:1–4
Gilgal	Jos 4:18–19
Shechem	Jos 8:30–35
Bethel	Jgs 20:27
Shiloh	1 Sm 3:3
Beth-Shemesh	1 Sm 6:13
Kiriath-jearim	1 Sm 7:1–2
Nob	1 Sm 22:11–16[7]
Jerusalem	2 Sm 6 ff.

For the above reasons we do not accept as historical the story of David's bringing the ark to Jerusalem as recorded in 2 Samuel 6. This is important to our understanding of the development of the religion of Israel. There were important theological concepts initiated by David when he made Jerusalem his capital. The impact of these concepts, however, was foreign to the Yahwistic worship of rural Israel during the historical reign of David. Only much later, with the passage of time, would the profound concepts of Zion theology and royal theology impact on the religious beliefs and practices of the farmers of rural Israel.

While the historicity of the story of David's transportation of the chest of Yahweh into Jerusalem may be questioned, there is a valuable dimension to the story that should not be overlooked. Large urban cult centers produced ceremonial processions. With a few strokes, the movement of the ark gives us an intriguing picture of what may have been processional practices in Davidic Jerusalem. J. W. Flanagan writes in *The New Jerome Biblical Commentary*.[8]

> [The story] abounds with signs of ritual: cultic music and dance, a procession, blessings and sacrifices, nudity and role reversals, all indicators of a rite of passage remembered in the Jerusalemite cult.

NOTES

1. There is no reference to the blind and the lame in Chronicles. Read Chronicles 11:4–9.

2. Gosta W. Ahlstrom, in his *History of Ancient Palestine* (pp. 470–71), suggests that Araunah was the last Jebusite king of Jerusalem.

3. Jerusalem, with David's extension to the north, was less than a half mile long and much narrower. With Solomon's further extension to the north to enclose the threshing floor, Jerusalem was only a mile long. The ancient city had a valley on three sides, west, south, and east. The north was not protected by a valley. So it was to the north that Solomon would expand the ancient, narrow city. See *NJBC*, pp. 1190–92.

4. A questioning of this assumption begins an article in *The Journal of Biblical Literature* (Summer 1994) by Karel van der Toorn and Cees Houtman, both of the Netherlands (p. 209). They write, "The logic which modern scholars perceive in David's action presupposes that the ark was the national symbol of the premonarchic tribes....this view must be challenged."

5. One of the indications that the ark narrative had accrued layers of authorship is the fact that there are three different names for the chest in 1 Samuel 4: the ark of God (El), the ark of the LORD (Yahweh), and the ark of

the covenant. Van der Toorn and Houtman, in their *SBL* article "David and the Ark," refer to the title "ark of the covenant" as a Deuteronomic appellation not in use before the time of Josiah (p. 226).

6. There may have been several chests at different locations where there were local sanctuaries—Gilgal, Shechem, Bethel, Shiloh, and Mizpah, for example. It is even possible to speculate that these cult objects may not have been chests but could have been images of animals similar to the bulls that Jeroboam is later said to have established at state sanctuaries, Bethel and Dan. The Josianic historian would have eliminated these unacceptable ancient local traditions from prestate Israel.

7. The chest (ark) of Yahweh is not specifically mentioned in this passage. There are several references to David making an enquiry of Yahweh at Nob with the assistance of Ahimelech the priest, the father of Abiathar. Abiathar later carries the chest (ark) in Jerusalem along with Zadok. Scholars van der Toorn and Houtman, in their article in *JBL* (Summer 1994), identify Nob as the location of an ark (chest) of divination during Saul's reign (pp. 227–31).

8. J. W. Flanagan's commentary on 2 Samuel, *NJBC*, p. 156.

9

Jerusalem Theology

Even though we have far more literary material in the Hebrew bible devoted to David than to any other king (forty-two chapters), we still have very little traditional historical narrative. Bracketed between "the Rise of David" (discussed in chapter 7) and the so-called court history, we have only eight chapters covering the rest of David's forty-year reign.[1]

In chapter 8 we questioned the historicity of the moving of the chest of Yahweh to Jerusalem as recorded in 2 Samuel 6. If there is reason to question the historicity of this event, there is even more reason to question the historicity of Nathan's conversation with David concerning the building of the temple and the establishing of a dynasty.

> ...the LORD declares to you that the LORD will make you a house....Your offspring...shall build a house for my name, and I will establish the throne of his kingdom forever. (2 Sm 7:11–13)

One of the practices of the Josianic historian (who put together the Deuteronomic history during the reign of Josiah) in establishing the traditional roles of prophets in Israel's history was to record conversations between prophets and kings.

The conversation between David and Nathan is followed by a so-called prayer of David. The prayer is not a prayer at all but one of a series of statements interspersed throughout the Deuteronomistic history to indoctrinate the reader/listener with the theology of the Deuteronomists. (It will be more appropriate for us to discuss Nathan's conversation with David and David's prayer when we turn to a later period in the development of Israel's theology.) Just as we must distinguish between Israel (historical) that produced the bible and Israel (theological) of the bible, so we must also distinguish between theology about David and David's actual religious beliefs and practices. The

CONVERSATIONS BETWEEN PROPHETS AND KINGS

A Literary Invention of the Josianic Historian

CHART 8

PROPHET	KING	LOCATION
Samuel	Saul	1 Sm 9:22
Nathan	David	2 Sm 7
Ahijah	Jeroboam	1 Kgs 11:29–39
Shemaiah	Rehoboam	1 Kgs 12:21
Jehu ben Hanani	Baasha	1 Kgs 16:14
Elijah	Ahab	1 Kgs 21:17–24
Micaiah	Jehoshaphat	1 Kgs 22:13–23
Isaiah	Ahaz	Is 7:25 [2]
Isaiah	Hezekiah	2 Kgs 20:1–19

idealization of David runs like a bright thread throughout the Deuteronomistic history. King after king of Judah is compared with David.

> Asa did what was right in the sight of the LORD, as his father David had done. (1 Kgs 15:11)

and

> He [Ahaz] did not do what was right in the sight of the LORD his God, as his ancestor David had done. (2 Kgs 16:2)

This idealism reaches its apex in Josiah.

> He [Josiah] did what was right in the sight of the LORD, and walked in all the way of his father David; he did not turn aside to the right or to the left. (2 Kgs 22:2)[3]

We do not doubt that David was a champion of Yahweh. But David was not a monotheist or a theologian. During his reign, other gods played a role in Jerusalem worship, including El, Baal, and Asherah.[4]

Priests Appointed by David

We read that David appointed priests:

> Zadok[5]...and Abiathar...were priests....and David's sons were priests. (2 Sm 8:18)

There are several interesting inferences here. First, the office of priest was held in high regard. Princes of the royal family became priests. Also, there was no tradition of a separate tribe of priests at that time.

The fact that a Judahite form of Yahweh worship was introduced into Jerusalem by David meant that an urban understanding of Yahweh would eventually develop. But many scholars believe that Jerusalem may have had an ancient unique theological heritage that would also play a vital role in the development of a royal cult. It is the role of Zadok, strangely enough, that gives us our first hint of Jebusite influence on the religion of Yahweh.

Unlike the other priest appointed by David—Abiathar, the son of Ahimelech—there is no previous mention of Zadok in the narrative of David before the acquisition of Jerusalem. Later, it is reported, Solomon banished Abiathar from Jerusalem (1 Kgs 2:26–27) because of his support of Adonijah as a successor to the throne of David. Some scholars have reached the conclusion that Zadok's appearance without a pre-Jerusalem reference indicates that he was a Jebusite priest of Jerusalem.[6]

Jerusalem and the Mountain of God

The acquisition of Jerusalem by David may have been the first identification of Yahweh with the mountain-of-God tradition. In Canaanite mythology a high god had a mountain. Did Yahweh have a mountain identification before his entry into Jerusalem? There are two possible answers, yes or no. Those who respond affirmatively point to the overwhelming impact of the recorded tradition of Israel's encounter with Yahweh at Sinai found in the book of Exodus. They also cite the references to Yahweh of Sinai found in several examples of ancient Hebrew poetry, Judges 5 and Psalm 68.[7]

> The mountains quaked before the LORD, the One of Sinai, before the LORD, the God of Israel. (Jgs 5:5)

> O God, when you went out before your people…the earth quaked, the heavens poured down rain at the presence of God, the God of Sinai. (Ps 68:7–8)

On the negative side there are several items to consider.

1. The location of Mount Sinai has not been agreed upon by scholars.[8]
2. Sinai is not specifically called a mountain in the ancient poetry. It was probably a wilderness area with a unique tradition located somewhere in the Sinai Peninsula. Thomas Dozeman, in a monograph entitled *God on the Mountain,* states that in the ancient poetry "Sinai is not a mountain but a region."[9]

3. In another scriptural tradition the area where Israel encountered Yahweh is called Horeb. Many feel that Horeb was an area (not a mountain) later identified with the Mount Sinai of Exodus.[10]

4. In spite of the very strong Sinai tradition (Israel's encounter with Yahweh at a mountain) of the canonical bible, it is possible that the Sinai tradition developed much later, after the acquisition of Jerusalem during (or after) the reign of David, and became inevitable as a result of David's introduction of Judean Yahwism into Jerusalem. Jerusalem had a Canaanite mountain-of-God tradition for several centuries before David's acquisition of it as a capital city.

5. In Joshua 24 there is a review of Israel's history with Yahweh. This review, of northern rural origin, is weak history but strong theology. Completely missing from this review (Joshua 24) is any reference to a Mount Sinai tradition. The Israelites move from Egypt to the wilderness to the promised land. Sinai is not mentioned.[11]

In coastal Canaan we have learned of a strong mountain-of-God tradition in the area of Sidon as a result of the Ras Shamra excavation.[12] In Psalms we have references to what scholars call Zion theology. The question is, does Zion theology combine old Canaanite traditions with David's Yahweh? Examples of Zion theology include

> Great is the LORD
> and greatly to be praised in the city of our God!
> His holy mountain, beautiful in elevation,
> is the joy of the whole earth,
> Mount Zion in the far north,[13]
> the city of the great king. (Ps 48:1–2)

and

> For the LORD has chosen Zion;
> He has desired it for his habitation:
> This is my resting place forever;
> here I will dwell for I have desired it....(Ps 132:13–14)

The discussion concerning whether Yahweh had a mountain connection before David obtained Jerusalem or whether he acquired a mountain only after entering Jerusalem as David's god will continue. What can be said with certainty is that the Jerusalem perception of Yahweh developed differently from the perception of Yahweh in northern rural shrines, such as Bethel and Shechem, and southern rural shrines, such as Beersheba.

Royal Theology

When David acquired Jerusalem he also laid the groundwork for what would develop as royal theology. In the ancient Near East, kingship was a sacred matter. Kings were regarded as directly related to the national god. The relationship ranged from the king being an adopted son of the god to the king being a god himself. In Israel the king would become an adopted son of Yahweh.

"I [Yahweh] have set my king on Zion, my holy hill....

You are my son; today I have begotten you." (Ps 2:6–7)

So the acquisition of Jerusalem would produce new understandings of the prestate Yahweh, and these new understandings would develop rather quickly (in a few decades) as the priests and theologians of David and Solomon worked to establish an Israelite national cult. It is important for us to remember that while this was happening, rural forms of Yahwism and Baalism continued to flourish outside of Jerusalem. It is reasonable to imagine that throughout Judah, former supporters of David were rewarded in various ways, and their continued support would make them more sensitive to the growth of a royal theology. This was not true in many rural shrines of Israel, the territory formerly ruled by the house of Saul.

Summary

The house of David was only able to rule the united kingdom for approximately eighty years. The acquisition of Jerusalem led to an understanding of the kingship of David's god Yahweh, a major theme of the Hebrew bible, a collection of scrolls that would have its origin in Jerusalem centuries after the period of the united kingdom. The mountain-of-God theology and Zion theology would continue to grow and develop in the small southern nation of Judah, and the house of David would survive until 587 B.C.E., more than a century after the destruction of Israel in the north. The Hebrew Bible was a product of Jerusalem, but important concepts from groups belonging to the northern tribes would play a decisive role in the emergence of scripture. But it was during the period of the united kingdom (the reigns of David and Solomon) that the theological merging of Yahweh with the institutions of monarchy and national political power first took place.

Before we turn to the north, there are some questions to ask concerning the reign of Solomon.

NOTES

1. Between the end of "the Rise of David" and the beginning of the court history, there are four chapters. Buried in the court history are four additional chapters that are out of place, 2 Samuel 21–24. Although we have forty-six chapters dealing with David, only eight are apart from two identifiable scrolls that may have had a life of their own apart from the Deuteronomistic history.

2. This conversation between Isaiah and Ahaz was not the invention of the Josianic historian. It appears only in the oracles of Isaiah of Jerusalem and may have been influential in suggesting to the historian the value of creating the literary form of a prophet speaking to a king.

3. This is the last mention of David in the books of Kings. The four kings following Josiah are not compared with David. This is one of the reasons many scholars believe that the first edition of the Deuteronomistic history ended with the reign of Josiah.

4. Gosta W. Ahlstrom, *The History of Ancient Palestine*, p. 477.

5. Ahlstrom makes an interesting comment about a scholarly reference to Zadok, that David would not have appointed a pagan as a high priest. Ahlstrom writes, "There were no pagans at that time" (p. 473).

6. For example, Rainer Albertz, *A History of Israelite Religion in the Old Testament Period* (Louisville, Ky.:Westminster/Knox, 1994), p. 129. Also J. Andrew Dearman, *Religion and Culture in Ancient Israel,* p. 66. For a discussion that raises questions about this conclusion, see *The New Jerome Biblical Commentary*, pp. 1256–57.

7. See Jon D. Levinson's book *Sinai and Zion* (Minneapolis: Winston Press, 1985), pp. 15–23.

8. Levinson uses this fact—that the location of Sinai is not pinpointed in the scripture—to bolster the idea that Sinai is supposed to function in no-man's-land and that the encounter between Israel and God was cosmic and extraterrestrial (pp. 19–23 of *Sinai and Zion*).

9. Thomas B. Dozeman, *God on the Mountain* (Atlanta: Scholars Press, 1989), p. 123.

10. There are seventeen references to Horeb in the Hebrew bible. Three times Horeb is called a mountain. In Exodus 3:1 we are told that Moses led the flock of his father-in-law Jethro "to Horeb, the mountain of God."

11. In the Deuteronomic scriptures the mountain of God is called Horeb. Some biblical historians believe that originally Horeb was not a mountain but an area. Martin Noth, in *A History of Pentateuchal Traditions* (Atlanta:

Scholars Press, 1981), speaks of our debt to von Rad who "convincingly demonstrated that the Sinai Tradition was an entity having its own origin and history, which was incorporated into the great corpus of the Pentateuchal tradition *secondarily* and *late*" (pp. 59–62).

12. Mount Zaphon was in Syria, north of Israel. It was believed to be the earthly counterpart of a heavenly Mount Zaphon where Baal had his castle built with El's permission.

13. Jerusalem was not in the far north, of course. Canaanite mythology located the home of the gods at Mount Zaphon, in the north.

10

The Reign of Solomon

There is no doubt that the Deuteronomic historian rewrote the history of Israel and in doing so, attempted to create a golden age when Yahweh was the only God of Israel. Because we, the readers, encounter Joshua first, we assume that the historian started with Joshua and his age as the counterbalance for the reforms of Josiah, which in fact would *reestablish* a solitary (monotheist) relationship between Yahweh and Yahweh alone as Israel's deserving ancient God. Although this was the form of the Josianic edition of DH, we cannot know in fact the stages through which the historian went to reach this outline.

It is at least possible that in an earlier draft of the history, the historian tried to make the golden age the reign of David. After first trying to follow this blueprint, the Josianic historian (or historians) may have decided that it would be more convincing, if the time and creative energy were available, to go back further into Israel's history and to begin the story with the capture of the land under the leadership of the Ephraimitic hero Joshua. As it is, the history has two models for Josiah, both Joshua and David.

The historian had two goals. The first goal was the establishment of Yahweh as the only God for Israel, and this goal was wed to the centralization theme that involved the city of Jerusalem. The historian knew that the religion of Jerusalem was polytheistic for centuries. According to his history, foreign gods were introduced in Jerusalem during the reign of Solomon. It may have been that the traditions of polytheistic worship in Jerusalem were so strong that they simply could not be ignored. But Solomon built the temple of Jerusalem and was the center of a wisdom tradition that named Yahweh as the grantor of this wisdom.

Two Periods of Solomon's Reign

So the historian decided to deal with the reign of Solomon by dividing it into two distinct periods. In the first period Solomon is as perfect as David. He prays for and is granted wisdom by Yahweh, he builds the temple with Yahweh's blessing, and he dedicates the temple with a great public prayer.

Of course, Solomon's prayer (1 Kgs 8) is not simply a prayer but, as it appears in DH, is a great Deuteronomistic statement. Many scholars believe that there are at least three levels of authorship in Solomon's dedication and prayer.[1]

The idealization of Solomon's reign ends in chapter 11, however. We are told that Solomon married many foreign wives. This was the cause of his downfall.

> For when Solomon was old, his wives turned away his heart after other gods; and his heart was not true to the LORD his God, as was the heart of his father David. (1 Kgs 11:4)

The use of the word *heart* three times in the above sentence reveals that this was the interpretation of the same circle that produced the book of Deuteronomy, where *heart* is a key word used repeatedly.

What does this tell us of the historical Solomon? It may tell us very little. By dividing the reign of Solomon into two periods, a pure period followed by a falling away from loyalty to Yahweh, the historian was able to state that Solomon built his Jerusalem temple solely for the worship of Yahweh. This may not have been the case. There is nothing about the Yahweh of Israel's pre-monarchic period that would lead us to believe that he desired a house for his resting place, as stated in Psalm 132.

> For the LORD hath chosen Zion;
> he has desired it for his habitation:
> "This is my resting place forever;
> here I will reside, for I have desired it." (Ps 132:13–14)

There was nothing Yahwistic about Solomon's temple. It was a copy of a Syrian structure built under the supervision of Phoenician craftsmen. The historian, knowing that Jerusalem was polytheistic throughout most of its history, created a pure period of Yahwistic devotion by having Solomon build the temple early in his reign while Solomon was still perfect like his father David. Solomon participated in the idealization of the reign of David. Complete and total devotion to Yahweh was vital to the historian's purpose of establishing Yahweh and Yahweh alone as the one god of Judah during the reign of Josiah, who

> ...did what was right in the sight of the LORD, and walked in all the way of his father David; he did not turn to the right or to the left. (2 Kgs 22:2)

The conversations between David and Nathan tied the construction of the temple firmly to the establishment of the Davidic dynasty. Scribes of Israel were fond of word play. In the story of Nathan and David there is a play on the word *house (bayith)*. David's offspring (Solomon) would build a house for the LORD, and the LORD would build a house (dynasty) for him (2 Sm 7:13–16). This story is pure theology. It legitimized Solomon's building of the temple.

The Divine Council

How did the gods of Jerusalem relate to each other? The bible's answer to this question is provided by references to a divine council. At first Yahweh was not the chief god of the council. An early reference is preserved for us in Deuteronomy 32.

> When the Most High (Elyon) apportioned the nations,
> when he divided humankind,
> he fixed the boundaries of the people according to
> the boundaries of the gods;
> Yahweh's own portion was his people,
> Jacob his allotted share. (Dt 32:8–9)

Later Yahweh would become the chief of the divine council.

> God has taken his place in the divine council;
> in the midst of the gods he holds judgement. (Ps 82:1)

> For who in the skies can be compared to the LORD?
> Who among the heavenly beings is like the LORD,
> a god feared in the council of the holy ones? (Ps 89:6–7)[2]

The Scroll of J

J is the letter used to identify one of the four sources of the Pentateuch. The other three are *E* (for El or Elohim), *P* (for the priest, or priestly), and *D* (for Deuteronomist). Many scholars believe that the scroll known as the work of J (the Yahwist or Jahwist) was produced during the reign of David or Solomon. If this is true, can we consult the scroll of J to determine the religious belief and practices of Solomon's reign? The answer is probably no for several reasons.

(a) The scroll of J was a court document with limited circulation. According to Robert Coote, in a recent book, *Early Israel,* "Only a tiny fraction of the people of Palestine knew what it said or cared."[3] In the canonical scriptures J begins with the creation of Adam, and later Eve, in the second chapter of Genesis. The work of J continues to be found in the Tetrateuch, ending in the book of Numbers with the blessing of Balaam.

(b) Scholars who believe that J was produced during the period of the united kingdom see the document (J) as a political work to create the impression that Israel's ancestors were nomadic sheikhs like Abraham, Isaac, and Jacob and not peasant farmers like the majority of the highland residents. The court of David needed the support of the tribal sheikhs of the Negev and the Philistine plain, and these supporters would identify with the patriarchs as opposed to the peasants of the highlands. Robert Coote writes:

> David's historian [was] an urban cleric [who] employed cuneiform sources originating in Mesopotamia rather than Palestinian folk traditions for his history of early humanity.[4]

(c) There are many scholars, however, who do not believe that the J document was a product of the united monarchy (tenth century). An increasing number believe that J was produced during the exile or during the Persian period of restoration a century after the death of Josiah.[5]

(d) Still others have set forth the view that there was no J document at all. The Yahweh of Genesis 2 who creates Adam and later Eve has little in common with the warrior god of premonarchic Israel. And the Yahweh who communicates with Abraham has even less in common with the warrior god. Further, the story of Joseph is recognized by some scholars to be an independent novella of the diaspora.[6]

Summary

The challenge that faces us in reviewing the period of the united kingdom and the developments of a Jerusalem form of Yahwism is to distinguish between the idealization of David and Solomon and the historical facts of the period.

There is no doubt that a completely new form of urban/royal Yahwism emerged in Jerusalem during the reign of David, to be further developed during the reign of Solomon. Assessing the influence of this hybrid on rural religious practices is more difficult. David and Solomon were faced with the challenge of creating a nation-state, and in so doing, their advisors, priests, court theologians, and scribes created a national cult. We cannot say with certainty that rural residents of Israel first became aware of the new national cult beliefs by contact with newly established state outposts such as storage cities.

> ...Solomon's storage cities, the cities of his chariots, the cities for his cavalry, and whatever Solomon desired to build in Jerusalem...and in all the land of his domination. (1 Kgs 9:19)

REASONABLE HISTORIC ASSUMPTIONS CONCERNING DAVID

CHART 9

1. During Saul's reign in the late eleventh century, David became chief of a large area south of Israel known as Judah.
2. Judah was not part of Saul's Israel.
3. Sometime after Saul's death, David was able to unite Israel and Judah into one monarchy.
4. David established the Jebusite city of Jerusalem as a neutral capital for the new monarchy.
5. David established a dynasty.
6. David was a champion of Yahweh.
7. A completely new form of Yahwism emerged in Jerusalem during the reigns of David and Solomon.

What we can be sure of is that all phases of rural life were touched and forever changed by the establishment of the Jerusalem monarchy. Residents throughout Israel would be influenced by economic and cultural changes that came with the establishment of Jerusalem as a capital city. Theological developments in Jerusalem were an integral part of the establishment of the new nation-state and, one way or another, could not long be ignored by clan elders and the leaders and priests of the diversified cult sites of rural Israel.

Both Jerusalem and the rural areas of Israel during the united kingdom period were polytheistic. So to blame the foreign wives of Solomon for the introduction of the worship of foreign gods in Jerusalem, suggesting that during the reign of David Yahweh was the sole god of Israel, is both oversimplified and misleading.

For the Josianic historian, on whom we are completely dependent, the presentation of David as the perfect servant of Yahweh, like Joshua, was of great theological importance. During his reign, David was never as popular with the people as the historian would have us believe.

It is entirely plausible, however, that David was a champion of Yahweh, the warrior god of the southern wilderness area, and that this Yahweh, after being introduced to the northern tribes by Hebrews who joined their numbers, was recognized throughout Israel as a champion of the lower classes of society, an ideal god for a marginal people. When Jerusalem began to see itself as a powerful city-state among the states of the Near East, a conception of a royal/urban Yahweh emerged. This Yahweh, interested in a temple and a throne, would hardly be recognizable as Yahweh as perceived by the rural masses of Israel.

With the death of Solomon, the united kingdom came to an end. It had lasted approximately eighty years (1000–922 B.C.E.). A new form of urban/ royal Yahwism existed in Jerusalem in embryonic form, but Jerusalem was polytheistic. Throughout Israel there was no unity in religious understanding and practice. There was no such thing as orthodoxy. In the rural areas of the north and at scattered sites in rural Judah, a variety of understandings concerning Yahweh and the Canaanite gods of fertility determined both community and family practices.

An interaction between rural and urban viewpoints would play a formative role in Israel's future giving birth to scriptural forms of biblical theology that would so greatly influence western civilization.

NOTES

1. Here is an example of the threefold authorship. The statement that the glory of the LORD filled the house and that the LORD desired to dwell in thick darkness (1 Kgs 8:11–12) is typical of the theology of Aaronid priests. The corrective statement that questions the thought expressed above with the words

> But will God indeed dwell on the earth? Even heaven and the highest heaven cannot contain you, much less this house that I have built…(8:27)

is Josianic and supplied by the Josianic historian. Exilic authorship could easily account for the prayers and pleadings of captive people who repent and call on Yahweh's mercy for deliverance (8:46–53).

2. Read 1 Kings 22:19–23 for a description of a divine council meeting.

3. Robert B. Coote, *Early Israel* (Minneapolis: Fortress, 1990), p. 155.

4. Robert Coote, p. 157.

5. J. van Seters in 1986 argued that J was an exilic product of the Persian period. See "The Yahwist as Historian," pp. 37–55 in *SBLSP* 25 (Atlanta: Scholars Press, 1986).

6. Donald Redford presents this view in several works, including *A Study of the Biblical Story of Joseph* (1970). See also Redford's book *Egypt, Canaan, and Israel in Ancient Times*, pp. 422–29.

Part III
ISRAEL IN THE NORTH
(922–722 B.C.E.)

11

The Northern Tribes Secede

> ...the assembly of Israel came and said to Rehoboam, "Your father made our yoke heavy. Now therefore lighten the hard service of your father [Solomon] and his heavy yoke that he placed on us and we will serve you." (1 Kgs 12:3)

Solomon and Statistics

Something we cannot fail to notice when reading about the reign of Solomon in the Deuteronomistic history is the large amount of statistics supplied to the reader. There is no other reign of a king of Judah or Israel described in the bible that has anything to compare with these numbers (see chart 10). The historian used many sources in producing DH, and the statistics concerning Solomon's monarchy probably came from a special source, "the Book of the Acts of Solomon" (1 Kgs 11:41).[1]

The statistics provided give us a picture of the bureaucracy and apparatus of state produced by the monarchical form of centralized government. The interrelationship of the social institutions of premonarchic rural Israel was no longer functional under the burdens of slave labor and taxation. Social institutions of premonarchic Israel were reconstellated. The center of social support shifted from the preservation of the extended family of agriculture to the preservation and support of an ever-expanding monarchy. The population of the capital city, Jerusalem, increased and the boundaries were extended. Food was no longer grown in Jerusalem or the immediate suburbs, so control of widespread agricultural areas became necessary. Administrative outposts for the monarchy and store cities were built with local slave labor. The cost of building these cities was paid by taxing the rural population of former subsistence farmers. Sons of farming families were conscripted for royal building projects. The demands of international trade promoted by Solomon took the

LEGENDARY NUMBERS INCLUDED IN THE ACCOUNT OF SOLOMON'S REIGN IN 1 KINGS

CHART 10

12,000	Horsemen	4:26
20,000	Cors of wheat sent to Hiram annually	5:11
30,000	Stout men	5:13
80,000	Stonecutters	5:15
70,000	Basket carriers	5:15
3,300	Supervisors	5:16
22,000	Oxen sacrificed on one occasion	9:63
120,000	Sheep sacrificed	9:63
666	Talents of gold (annual income)	10:14
1,400	Chariots	10:26
700	Wives	11:3
300	Concubines	11:3

NOTE: The above statistics were not produced in the primary source as a criticism of Solomon. The purpose of these numbers was to boast of the splendor of Solomon's reign. Produced in a prescientific age, there is no reason to take the statistics literally. For example, it has to be folklore that Solomon had seven hundred wives. Even if these numbers are substantially reduced, they still give us a hint of the burdens placed on the rural population of Israel and the changes that took place in their way of life.

decisions concerning crops out of the hands of the farmers. The demand for grain, oil, and wine increased for trade purposes, and the workers were able to keep only a small portion of their output.

While life became comfortable and luxurious for the residents of Jerusalem, life became unbearable for the residents of the northern areas. David had had some understanding of the hardships of life for rural people, but Solomon led a sheltered life from his birth and had the makings of the ideal tyrant. It could be said that Solomon reduced the independent farmers of the northern clans to the status of Hebrews. Independent cultivators became tenants and debt slaves. Robert Coote writes,

Solomon was a home-grown pharaoh, a son of Israel in name only.[2]

While we are getting ahead of our story, it is interesting at this point to look at the only portion of law that mentions the king, found in a body of law of northern origin (now found in Dt 12–26). The particular law forbids the king from having too many horses, too many wives, and too much gold.

> Even so, he [the king] must not acquire many horses for himself....And he must not acquire many wives for himself...also silver and gold he must not acquire in great quantity for himself. (Dt 17:16-17)

It was David who began the economic exploitation of the rural residents of the northern tribes, the area previously ruled by Saul, but it was Solomon who carried the exploitation to extremes and made the revolt and secession of the north following his death inevitable.

Discontent in the North

In David's declining years, we are told, some of the people of Israel tried to revolt under the leadership of Sheba, a Benjaminite.

> Now a scoundrel named Sheba son of Birchi, a Benjaminite...sounded the trumpet and cried out "We have no portion with David,
> No share in the son of Jesse!
> Everyone to your tents O Israel!"
> (2 Sm 20:1)

Although Sheba is identified as a Benjaminite (the tribe of Saul), Joab later identifies Sheba as a man of the hill country of Ephraim (2 Sm 20:21). We don't know much about the rebellion led by Sheba, but we have these words attributed to David:

> Now Sheba son of Birchi will do us more harm than Absalom. (2 Sm 20:6)

David considered the revolt a major crisis. He sent Joab's men and the warriors of Judah, along with the Cherethites and the Pelethites, to pursue him. The historian Ahlstrom, commenting on the united kingdom, writes,

> The unity between the different parts of the kingdom was forced and artificial. In contrast to Judah, the people of the north, Israel,

had been treated as a vassal nation after Sheba's uproar. The harsh treatment, including forced labor and hard taxation, backfired.[3]

Because the Josianic historian wanted to minimize this revolt, many details are omitted. But the rebellion of Sheba, along with reference to the arguments between the men of Judah and the men of Israel (2 Sm 19:41-43), gives us an indication of the discontent growing in the north during the reign of David. Forty years later, following the death of Solomon, the alienation of the northern clans was complete.

Shechem

Considering the fractured topography of the northern area and the geographically fragmented regions, it is surprising that the areas could unite to the degree they did in their dispute with Solomon's son, Rehoboam. We are told, surprisingly, that Rehoboam[4] had to travel to Shechem to negotiate for his throne. Shechem was located in the valley between Mount Gerazim and Mount Ebal and in past times had been a major Canaanite cult center. It was almost thirty miles from Jerusalem, so Rehoboam had to make a long journey to meet with representatives of Israel's clans. A glance at the map of Israel shows that Shechem was a central location in the Ephraimite hill country and centrally located for the northern clans. It may indicate that in the minds of the Israelites, new boundaries had already been drawn, with Judah omitted, and that the meeting with Rehoboam was a last-ditch effort of the north to stay with Judah.

In Deuteronomy Shechem is identified as a location where the united tribes, following the directions of Moses, built a large altar of unhewn stones for Yahweh. Here there was no vast Syrian temple for Yahweh, such as the one Solomon built in Jerusalem.

The Ascendancy of Yahweh in the North

If the Solomonic administration treated the rural residents of Israel like Hebrews, it is possible that the god the Hebrews introduced to the northern clans, Yahweh, a god of war perceived as one who would fight for and defend the powerless and lowly, increased in importance among the diverse gods recognized in rural Israel. Remembering that Israelites were originally the indigenous people of the land of Canaan, who moved into the hill country (later called Israel) from all directions, we have to remind ourselves that there was no uniformity of religious belief and practice such as that represented for us in the canonical scriptures.

But throughout history oppression by a common enemy has frequently increased unity in oppressed people, and it is our suggestion that an increase of the importance of Yahweh as a functional god for the northern clans took place in a decisive way during the eighty years of the united kingdom. This emerging understanding of Yahweh in the north would differ from the right turn that the understanding of David's Yahweh took in the royal capital city of Jerusalem.

The important characteristic Jerusalemite beliefs of the canonical scriptures, with which the student is very familiar, would not have been part of the Yahweh worship of the north at centers such as Bethel, Shiloh,[5] Gilgal, Shechem, Taanach, or Megiddo. For example:

(a) Yahweh would not be seen as a god who chose Jerusalem as a place for his dwelling or for his name to dwell.

(b) Yahweh would not have desired a large house or temple.

(c) Yahweh would not have been understood as the counterpart of an earthly king.

(d) Yahweh would not have been bound to the dynasty of David forever.

(e) In the north Yahweh may not as yet have been connected with a mountain-of-God tradition. A northern tradition has Israel encountering Yahweh at Horeb (Dt 1:6 and 5:2). Horeb may have originally been an area rather than a mountain.

Who Was Jeroboam?

Of the major persons of the bible, Jeroboam is the number-one candidate for flatness. Considering that Jeroboam was the first king of Judah's sister nation to the north, that Jeroboam led a revolution against the house of David, and also that Jeroboam was repeatedly blamed for the rejection of Israel by Yahweh and its final destruction (722 B.C.E.), Jeroboam comes across as an uninteresting, two-dimensional character. The reason for this is that Jeroboam the person is completely buried under the theology of the Josianic historian. None of Jeroboam's humanity comes through to the reader. For a leader of a revolution as important as the secession of Israel from Judah to be so bloodless demands an intentional contempt on the part of the historian.

The material covering Jeroboam, as we have it, is almost wholly dedicated to the theological belief that the relationship of the king to Yahweh completely determines the fate of the nation. Examples of this viewpoint are many. Israel is ripped from Solomon's son because Solomon's heart is turned from Yahweh by his foreign wives. Judah is later destroyed by the neo-Babylonians (in spite of Josiah's righteousness and reforms) because of the wickedness of Manasseh. Jeroboam is repeatedly referred to as the one who made Israel to sin.

The puzzle is that Jeroboam's acts in establishing Bethel and Dan as Israelite shrines with the erection of a bull calf at each site did not constitute a rejection of Yahweh by Jeroboam.[6] But the historian reports that the prophet Ahijah, speaking for Yahweh, declares,

> ...but you [Jeroboam] have done evil above all those who were before you and have gone and made for yourself other gods, and cast images, provoking me to anger, and have thrust me behind your back. (1 Kgs 14:9)

So we are told in DH that the northern kingdom is doomed from the start because Jeroboam turned from Yahweh and erected two calves (young bulls), one at Dan and the other at Bethel, and declared that these locations were the official shrines of Israel. Jeroboam is also blamed for building and tolerating high places *(bamoth),* even though high places (scattered shrines used as places of worship, frequently but not always on hills) were common and acceptable in Israelite history (including the period throughout each monarchy) until the discovery of the Book of the Law during the reign of Josiah.[7]

Contempt for Jeroboam

It is the belief of this author that we have to read between the lines to determine the particular contempt the historian had for Jeroboam. The Deuteronomic circle, which produced DH, traced its heritage to Shechem, and happenings at Shechem during the early days of Jeroboam's reign determined his place in the canonical bible. Jeroboam reigned for twenty-two years, but we know almost nothing about his administration. What we do know, however, is revealing. We know that Jeroboam was crowned at Shechem, and shortly thereafter "...he went out from there and built Penuel."

Shechem was the location of a major Yahwistic shrine, cared for and operated by a circle of priests who considered themselves Levites. When Jeroboam moved from Shechem to Penuel, we are told,

> ...he [Jeroboam] appointed priests from among the people who were not Levites. (1 Kgs 12:31)

And later

> Jeroboam...made priests for the high places again from among the people; any who wanted to be priests he consecrated for the high places. (1 Kgs 13:33)

Notice the derogatory words "any who wanted to be priests." In DH the priesthoods of Israel, the northern kingdom, are thus identified as illegitimate priesthoods.[8] To understand the so-called sins of Jeroboam, which all the kings of

Israel are accused of perpetuating, we have to look through the eyes of the Deuteronomic circle. Jeroboam rejected the priests of Shechem by moving his monarchy, first to Penuel and later to Tizrah. When he established Bethel as a national shrine site, Bethel became competition not only for Jerusalem but also for Shechem. In the circle of Yahwistic priests of Shechem, Jeroboam became frozen as a symbol of Yahweh rejection, a symbol that would survive for centuries for the descendants of the Shechem cult leaders. In the next chapter we will speculate on the further significance of the establishment of Dan and Bethel as the official shrines of the new nation.

NOTES

1. It is interesting to note that many bible historians and scholars raise many doubts in their writings about the historical facts concerning various kings, including Solomon, but then proceed to use the numbers provided during the description of Solomon's reign as factual.

2. *In Defense of Revolution*, p. 59.

3. Ahlstrom, *The History of Ancient Palestine*, p. 543.

4. In spite of the large amount of statistics we are given concerning Solomon, it is interesting to note that we are not supplied with the names of his wives or any of his children except Rehoboam and his mother. We become aware that the material concerning David differs from the traditional material preserved for Solomon.

5. While many scholars believe that a temple building was destroyed at Shiloh by the Philistines around 1050, it is possible that Israelite cultic activity continued in the area following this incident.

6. Almost all scholars agree that Jeroboam established shrines for the worship of Yahweh, as Yahweh was widely perceived by Israelites during the tenth century. The bull calf was a symbol of both El and Yahweh. Jerome Walsh writes in the *NJBC*, "Jeroboam clearly intends to establish sanctuaries of Yahweh" (p. 169). See also Ahlstrom's *History of Ancient Palestine*, pp. 552-53. See also Susan Ackerman, *Every Green Tree*, p. 174.

7. Read Deuteronomy 12.

8. Later we will discuss the further corruption of the priesthood of Bethel by the Assyrians in 2 Kings 17:24-34.

12

Bethel and Dan

> So the king [Jeroboam] took counsel, and he made two calves of gold. He said to the people, "You have gone up to Jerusalem long enough. Here are your gods, O Israel, who brought you out of the land of Egypt." He set one in Bethel and the other he put in Dan.
> (1 Kgs 12:28–29)

Although we are told that Jeroboam established two national shrines, we hear nothing about activity at Dan in the Deuteronomistic history. The reason for this is that Dan was far from Jerusalem. Dan was in the far north of Israel on the Syrian border (parallel with the seaport of Tyre). The historian has no interest in the religious activities of Dan. Archaeological excavation has confirmed Dan as an active cultic site in the ninth century. Incense stands, a horned altar, an olive press, and a large stone platform near a spring that fed the Jordan River have been uncovered.[1]

Bethel, like Dan, was a border shrine, on the southern border of Israel/Judah, and because of its close proximity to Jerusalem, it became the favorite target for the historian. Bethel, unlike nearby Jerusalem (eleven miles to the south) had a strong premonarchical Yahweh tradition.[2] For many years Bethel had been a favorite holy place for the farmers of Ephraim. It was one of the towns in Samuel's circuit (1 Sm 7:16) and a place to which Israelites carried offerings (1 Sm 10:3). Genesis preserves for us a Jacob/Bethel tradition where Jacob, fleeing from Esau, dreams of a ladder from earth to heaven and declares, "Surely Yahweh is in this place—and I did not know it....This is none other than the house of God, and this is the gate of heaven." Later Jacob is instructed to build an altar at Bethel to the God who had appeared to him.

In spite of this, the altar at Bethel is condemned severely as an abomination to Yahweh, not only in DH (1 Kgs 13:1–6 and 2 Kgs 23:15–20), but also in Deuteronomic additions to the oracles of both Amos and Hosea.[3] The historian succeeds in putting Bethel in the worst possible light.

But the historian misleads us concerning the religious practices of Bethel, the southern national shrine of the northern kingdom. In spite of its premonarchic Yahwistic tradition, the reader of (or the listener to) the Deuteronomistic history is led to believe that Jeroboam introduced a new, abominable practice to Israel when he constructed the two golden bull calves. This was not true. The bull as a symbol had long been connected with many deities of Canaan, including El, Baal, and Yahweh.[4] It was a familiar symbol to many residents of the northern kingdom.

The student of the bible cannot read of the golden calves of Jeroboam without thinking of the sin of Aaron in making a golden calf while Moses was delayed on Mount Sinai during his reported encounter with God (Ex 32). Scholars are divided over the determination of whether the story of Aaron's particular disobedience in making a golden calf had an existence before Jeroboam. Many conclude that the account of Aaron's calf evolved later than the account of Jeroboam's action, to project into Israel's ancient history a polemic against Jeroboam's calves. Martin Noth and others state that the two accounts (Aaron and Jeroboam) were written by the same author.[5]

In understanding the diversity of Yahweh worship in ancient Israel, it is helpful to understand the history of Jeroboam's reputation in DH. It is our contention that Jeroboam's infamy began when he split with the leaders of the cult of Yahweh at Shechem. The reasons Jeroboam moved from Shechem, his first royal city, to Penuel and later to Tirzah, are not commented on by the historian.[6] We are told, however, that Jeroboam did not accept the priests of Shechem but, upon choosing a new location for his monarchy, immediately appointed priests from among the people who were not Levites. Jeroboam continued his avoidance of Levitical priests when he established Bethel and Dan as national shrines and when he built further high places *(bamoth)*. It is possible that it was with his split with the cult leaders of Shechem that the reputation of Jeroboam as an evil enemy of Yahweh originated. The priests and scribes of Shechem were among the early producers of scrolls, and when their descendants, influenced by the ancient theology of Shechem, later produced the bible's first history of Israel (DH) to support and promote the Josianic reforms of centralization and standardization of Yahweh worship in Jerusalem, Jeroboam had already been clearly established as the individual responsible for the sins of Israel.[7] These sins were responsible for the tragic events of 722, when the Assyrians destroyed Samaria and put an end to the nation Israel.

> …Israel continued in all the sins that Jeroboam committed; they did not depart from them until the LORD removed Israel out of his sight. (2 Kgs 17:22)

The Historic Jeroboam

Jeroboam reigned for twenty-two years, and although it is difficult for the modern student of the bible to imagine it, he may have been an excellent first king for the newly established monarchy (or reestablished monarchy, if we consider Saul the first king) of the nation Israel. There is a benefit for the student in understanding this possibility. It has little to do with fairness, however. The theological misunderstanding of Jeroboam contributes to the belief that there was indeed an invalid understanding of Yahweh at Bethel and that this particular form of heresy was prevalent throughout Israel. There are two things wrong with this assumption: (1) Historically nothing could be further from the truth than that the fall of Israel to the Assyrians in 722, led by Shalmaneser V and Sargon II, was the fault of Jeroboam's form of Yahwism, and (2) all Israel did not follow Jeroboam. There were many understandings of Yahweh and multiple cults of Yahweh in Israel. The conflict between Shechem and Bethel was only one of several possible conflicts. As we have stated, there were cults of Yahweh in many locations throughout Israel, including Megiddo, Gilgal, Taanach, Shiloh,[8] and of course, Shechem. And there was no one authority or overseer to define orthodoxy or say which belief or practice was true and valid. As we have stated earlier in this study, the phrase *all Israel* is at best misleading in describing the culture of the northern kingdom until the idealization of Israel's past began, probably during the reign of Hezekiah.

We cannot leave Jeroboam without noting the phrase attributed to him when he constructed his bull calves at Dan and Bethel.

> Here are your gods,[9] O Israel, who brought you up out of the land
> of Egypt. (1 Kgs 12:28)

The promotion of the exodus tradition, reminding the people of their deliverance from slave labor shortly after the split with Rehoboam, seems quite a wise move on Jeroboam's part and not the type of action the historian would have fabricated for Jeroboam, considering the picture the historian was trying to present of him. The exodus reference argues for a genuine Jeroboam tradition of ancient origin. Rainer Albertz writes, in *A History of Israelite Religion in the Old Testament Period,*

> ...the golden bull image was to symbolize the unbounded power
> of Yahweh as god of the Exodus and liberator from the oppression
> of Egypt—and Solomon. And it was to demonstrate that the
> national cult of the North was the real heir of the old Yahweh tra-
> ditions as opposed to the Jerusalem innovations. Yahweh was to
> be worshipped in Bethel, not as the god-king enthroned on Zion,

fighting against chaos, creator of the world and ruler of nations, but as the one who liberates his people from Egypt. (p. 145)

The Worship of Multiple Gods

As the period of the two monarchies began, we had two national forms of Yahwism, one in Judah and one in Israel. They differed from each other. But both of these national forms of Yahweh worship had something in common. Neither excluded the worship of other gods. In Jerusalem even the historian admits that foreign gods were worshiped. In Samaria we know that there was a temple for Baal. In both Israel and Judah El was not completely differentiated from Yahweh, and although DH does not reveal much about it, the worship of Asherah as an independent goddess and as a consort of Yahweh was widely accepted.

We do ourselves a disservice when we use such terms as *foreign, Canaanite,* and *pagan* to describe the national religious practices of the post-Solomonic period. Later we will have more to say about the recognition of these gods (El, Asherah, Baal). They were indigenous throughout the area of Palestine and Syria. But we are suggesting that during the period of the united kingdom (the reign of David and Solomon), Yahweh moved to a more prominent position in the circle of national gods for two unrelated reasons. In Jerusalem Yahweh was promoted by David because David had personally credited Yahweh with his rise to power. David championed the cause of the warrior god he encountered in the southern wilderness area of the Negev when he, David, was a warrior himself. In Israel Yahweh increased in importance during the reign of Solomonic oppression and exploitation bordering on slavery when the Israelites remembered the god introduced to them by the Hebrew survivors of a historical exodus experience of deliverance from slavery.

NOTES

1. See the *NJBC*, p. 1198 and 1213. Also, see *B.A.R.,* March-April, 1994, pp. 38-39.

2. There are some vague connections of Yahweh with Jerusalem that claim to be ancient (premonarchic), but these are considered to be of postexilic origin. See Albertz, *A History of Israelite Religion*, p. 308.

3. The altar at Bethel is condemned five times in the Josianic edition of the book of Amos, and it is in Bethel that Amos confronted the high priest Amaziah and spoke scathing words of renunciation of King Jeroboam II (Am 7:10–17). Hans W. Wolff, in *Joel and Amos* (Philadelphia: Fortress Press, 1984), identifies references to Bethel in Amos as chiefly from the Josianic

exposition of Amos (pp. 111–12). Also, Grace Emerson, in her book *Hosea, An Israelite Prophet in a Judean Perspective*, states that the name Bethaven in Hosea 4:15—

> Do not enter into Gilgal,
> or go up to Bethaven

—means "house of shame" and was a contemptuous name for the sanctuary at Bethel (p. 136).

4. See Ahlstrom, *History of Ancient Palestine*, p. 553. Many scholars, feeling uncomfortable with the identification of Yahweh with the bull image, stress the fact that the bull was only a pedestal upon which God stood. These scholars include W. F. Albright and R. de Vaux.

5. Noth, *Exodus* (Philadelphia: Fortress, 1962), p. 246. Also, Ahlstrom, in his *History*, states that "…it is likely that they [both accounts] were written by the same person."

6. We contend that it was a practice of the Deuteronomic historian(s) to keep a low profile and not to reveal details of their own history (the Levitical priestly circle of Shechem). For this reason we find that there are several places in the history where we would want more information, which is not supplied to us. We remind ourselves that although Bethel was a competing shrine for Jerusalem for the length of Israel's existence and even afterward (2 Kgs 17:24–28), Shechem also was a competing shrine for Jerusalem until the destruction of the northern kingdom. Reminding the reader of this would have been counterproductive for the Josianic goals of the Deuteronomic circle.

7. For a further discussion of this viewpoint, see the author's book *Obsession with Justice: The Story of the Deuteronomists*, pp. 25–32.

8. Although it is widely believed that Shiloh as a major shrine was destroyed by the Philistines in 1050 B.C.E., it is possible that cult activity resumed in the Shiloh area during the period of the united monarchy.

9. The historian does not seem to be accusing Jeroboam of polytheism by using the word *gods*. The word refers to the two bull calves at the two sites, Dan and Bethel.

13

High Places

And so we conclude that the construction of the two bull calves by Jeroboam did not become a horrible sin until a century or so later, after the fact. The strong condemnatory statement attributed to Yahweh through (i.e., spoken by) Ahijah the prophet was not spoken during the lifetime of Jeroboam. The statement was written centuries later.

> …you have done evil above all those who were before you and have gone and made for yourself other gods; and cast images, provoking me to anger, and have thrust me behind your back. (1 Kgs 14:9)

But since the Josianic historian (or an exilic editor) was committed to the full condemnation of Jeroboam, he also decided to mention Jeroboam's relationship to the high places.

> Jeroboam also made houses on high places. (1 Kgs 12:31)

In another location in DH the people are blamed for using the high places.

> The people of Israel secretly[1] did things that were not right against the LORD their God. They built for themselves high places at all their towns, from watchtower to fortified city. (2 Kgs 17:9)

Chronology of the Historian

The northern kingdom endured for two hundred years, from 922 to 722 B.C.E. The Josianic historian gives us a sketchy account of the history of Israel by interweaving it with his account of Judah, switching back and forth from the north (Israel) to the south (Judah). The historian must be given credit for his attempt to keep a chronology constantly before the reader of this history. For example, to begin his chronology, he tells us that Jeroboam reigned for twenty-two years and that Rehoboam, in Jerusalem, reigned for seventeen years. This informs the reader that Jeroboam was still king of Israel when Rehoboam's son Abijam became king of Judah.

> Now in the eighteenth year of King Jeroboam son of Nebat, Abijam began to reign over Judah. (1 Kgs 15:1)

The historian continues this interweaving for the entire two hundred years of Israel's existence. This gives the reader the feeling that the historian is presenting objective facts. While the historian contributed much to our understanding of the history of Israel, he was primarily a theologian. In producing his magnificent history of Israel and Judah, he never lost sight of his primary goal, which was to present a theological interpretation of Israel's past. According to this theology, the northern kingdom deserved to be destroyed.[2] The tragic events of 722 (of course, the historian did not use this date) were the inevitable results of Israel's sins (and/or Jeroboam's sins) against Yahweh. At the beginning of Israel's history, we were told that Jeroboam made houses on *high places*. At the end of Israel's history, as the historian gives us a résumé of Israel's sins (2 Kgs 17:7–18), we are told that the people[3] built high places at all their towns.

What Was a High Place?

The high place *(bama)* was a place where cultic activity was engaged in. Many people of a city or town (any city or town) or other identifiable area would gather at the local high place for a number of reasons. Before we look at the activities of a high place we will list some interesting facts.

(1) The term *high place* is a generic term for an appealing, convenient, and appropriate location for public cultic activity.
(2) High places were frequently but not necessarily on high plateaus.[4]
(3) Some high places were open-air sanctuaries with no buildings.
(4) Archaeologists have unearthed large stone platforms at *bamoth* sites, approximately six feet high and twenty-five feet wide.[5]
(5) Frequently there was a building or temple at the high place.
(6) High places had altars for sacrifices.
(7) It was an advantage for a high place to have a history or tradition. Bethel had a tradition as the location where Jacob had his dream (Gn 28:10–22).
(8) High places in highly populated areas were staffed by priesthoods.
(9) In addition to altars on platforms, there were other constructions at high places, including pillars and sacred poles.
(10) Israel did not invent high places. High places were the popular worship

centers for Canaanite farmers for centuries before Israel became a nation-state.

Were There Priesthoods at High Places?

Our understanding is that a high place was any place (frequently but not always an elevated area) where people gathered for cultic activity.[6] There were too many high places to count. We can assume that in densely populated areas, high places would support and require the activity of a professional priesthood. In sparsely populated areas, elders of the community would perform priestly activity when required. It is even possible that a large isolated family could have its own high place, a family cult location in which an elder of the family would serve as a priest.[7]

Later, when we discuss the religious practices of Judah following the destruction of the northern kingdom (722), we will note that there were priests in many of the forty-six towns and villages of Judah during the reign of Josiah.[8]

Solomon and the Great High Place at Gibeon

It is interesting to note that an important tradition involving Solomon at a high place refers to the rite of incubation and that incubation seems not to have been condemned in the body of law associated with the Josianic reforms.[9] The participation of kings in incubation rites is widely reported in the literature of the ancient Near East.[10] It consisted of the following: The king or supplicant would present himself at a sacred place for the occasion and make sacrifices to the god whose favor was sought and with whom a dream encounter was desired. Occasionally fasting preceded the sacrifices. The supplicant would sleep at the sacred place. If the deity appeared in a dream encounter, the supplicant would make a request. When the dreamer returned to his home, additional sacrifices were made to the god. The rite frequently ended with a sign from the god that the supplicant's request had been granted. The fact that the supplicant would go to a special location for the dream encounter indicates that Israelites believed that certain locations were particularly holy and favored by a god.

The site of Solomon's dream encounter was Gibeon, referred to as the principal high place.

> The king went to Gibeon to sacrifice there, for that was the principal high place. (1 Kgs 3:4)

This is not the only biblical passage that reveals to us that activity at high places was considered legitimate. Samuel and Saul participated in a sacrificial meal at a high place with thirty others (1 Sm 9:11–26).

The Multiplicity of High Places

Since the goal of the Deuteronomic circle during the reign of Josiah (640–609) was the centralization and standardization of a particular form of Yahweh worship in Jerusalem, the multiplicity of high places was considered by the Josianic historian as intolerable, and their elimination was absolutely necessary and in the best interests of the people of Judah. The great evil of multiple high places was projected into Israel's past. The elimination of multiple cultic sites was the center of the historian's theological program.[11]

The Activities of High Places

We will list the activities that Israelites engaged in during the length of the nation-state's existence, 922 to 722 B.C.E. These practices were common both in the north and the south, in both rural and urban areas. For several reasons we have decided to deal with Judah separately. Judah, the southern nation, survived for more than a century following the destruction of Israel, and reformer priests living in Jerusalem (or exiled Judahites following the destruction of Jerusalem) produced the Hebrew scrolls that identify the activities at high places.

Most of the practices we will list were later specifically condemned in the canonical Hebrew bible. As modern students we have been sensitized by twenty-four centuries of what has been called the Judeo-Christian heritage, and because we live in an age of science, many of the activities listed will repulse our sensitivities and offend what we now call our common sense. But for the ancient Israelites these practices were in accord with their understanding of the world and its gods. They are not to be harshly condemned because they did not know better. We can keep in mind that from their number several groups emerged that eventually did condemn and purge offensive Israelite practices and consequently produced the profound ethical theology that has endured for millennia and still shapes and forms our ethics and morals today and engages the minds of our best theological scholars. But more about this later.

The Deuteronomistic history contains a narrative description of the sins of Israel (the northern kingdom) to explain why Yahweh had destroyed Israel in 722 (2 Kgs 17:7–18). This list must be used with caution, however. While it claims to describe the practices of the northern kingdom, the form in which it appears is obviously edited by an exilic editor (587–539 B.C.E.). We must remember the following: (1) The historian(s) was (were) more interested in cultic purity than historical accuracy. (2) This list of abominable practices may have first appeared during the reign of Josiah, one hundred years after the destruction of the northern kingdom. (3) Its Josianic version was directed to reforms needed in Judah and may more accurately have described the practices of Judean high places.

Nevertheless, the historian takes pains to distinguish between Judah and Israel (2 Kgs 17:18–20). Since the practices of high places in Judah must have had their counterpart in Israel, we will use the list with reservations.

(1) They made offerings at multiple high places.
(2) They erected pillars (*massebim*, v. 10).
(3) They erected sacred poles (*asherim*, v. 10).
(4) They served idols (v. 12).
(5) They made their sons and daughters pass through the fire (v. 17).
(6) They worshiped all the host of heaven (v. 16).
(7) They used divination and sorcery (v. 17).
(8) They served Baal (v. 16).
(9) They did wicked things "under every green tree and on every high hill" (v. 11).

Our first reservation is this. It does not accurately and completely describe all forms of cultic activity in Israel from 922 to 722 B.C.E. Also, by our assumption that there was no widespread uniformity throughout Israel, activities at some high places differed from the activities of other high places. But it is necessary for us to understand high-place activity in greater detail than that supplied by the Josianic historian.[12]

All high places had outdoor altars for animal sacrifices. These altars were made of unhewn stones and had pointed projections, or mini-mountain-shaped horns, at the four corners. These corners may have prevented the animal being sacrificed from slipping off the altar.

There were frequently two phallic symbols next to the altars, a pillar *(massebah)* and a sacred pole *(ashera)*. The stone pillar was a symbol for male genitalia and the sacred pole (a real tree or a stylized tree) was a symbol of female genitalia. In the Josianic reforms the stone pillars are smashed and the trees (sacred poles) are cut down, uprooted, or burned.[13] A Deuteronomic law warns the people of seventh-century Judah,

> You shall not plant any tree as an *asherah* beside the altar that you make for Yahweh your god. (Dt 16:9)

The wicked things the people did were no doubt associated with sexual activity, including sacred sexual intercourse. Fertility cult activity is not dwelt on in the Hebrew scrolls, but some specific references are available. A verse in Hosea reads:

> They sacrifice on the tops of the mountains,
> and make offerings upon the hills,
> under oak, poplar, and terebinth,

because their shade is good.
Therefore your daughters play the whore,
and your daughters-in-law commit adultery. (Hos 4:13)[14]

Concerning divination and sorcery, there is little doubt that the farmers
of Israel believed in these powers and procedures whereby the will of a god
could be determined and his or her blessing sought. Sometimes blessings were
sought for loved ones or self, or curses for enemies. Communication with the
dead was related to divination. A tradition of Saul states that he had expelled
the mediums and the wizards from the land (1 Sm 28:3). In Deuteronomic law
divination is grouped under the heading "the abhorrent practices of those
nations" (Dt 18:9).[15]

It is probable that the priests of the high places were always men, and if
a woman felt that she was gifted in the area of divination or was believed by
others to possess this gift, she would offer her services independently, in her
own home. These independents (which in some cases could be men) were
identified as witches, wizards, or mediums, and their activity was condemned
by certain laws. A law in the collection usually called the Book of the
Covenant states,

You shall not permit a female sorcerer to live. (Ex 22:18)[16]

Child Sacrifice

There is no doubt that the canonical Hebrew bible condemns child sacrifice
unequivocally. Both priestly law (Lv 18:21, 20:2–5) and Deuteronomic law
(Dt 12:31, 18:10–12) prohibit this gruesome and horrible practice. But other
scripture reveals that to some extent child sacrifice was practiced in Judah.
The Deuteronomistic historian reports that King Ahaz of Judah (during the
lifetime of Isaiah nevertheless)

...walked *in the way of the kings of Israel.* He even made his son
pass through fire, according to the abominable practices of the
nations whom the LORD drove out before the people of Israel.
(2 Kgs 16:3)

We are also informed that Manasseh (also of Judah) made his son pass through
the fire. It is interesting to note that the two kings singled out for this condemnation were both Judean and that no king of Israel is cited. Also, no location in
Israel is identified as a place of child sacrifice.

We are later informed that as part of the reforms of Josiah,

He defiled Topheth…so that no one would make a son or a daughter pass through fire as an offering to Molech. (2 Kgs 23:10)

Molech (also Moloch) was a god of the Ammonites imported from the region of the middle Euphrates (Malik or Milcom?). In his old age Solomon is said to have built an altar for Milcom, under the influence of his Ammonite wives.

A passage in Jeremiah condemns the people of Judah.

And they go on building the high places of Topheth…to burn their sons and their daughters in the fire—which I did not command, nor did it come into my mind. (Jer 7:31)

The scripture references above indicate child sacrifice in Judah, and in this chapter we are examining practices of the northern kingdom of Israel. We have brought up the subject of child sacrifice because the historian lists this practice as one of the reasons for the destruction of Israel in 722 by the Assyrians (2 Kgs 17:17).[17]

Summary

The reader (or listener) of DH is given a list of activities at high places as an explanation for the destruction of the northern kingdom by Assyria in 722 (2 Kgs 17). But the list in its present form appears in an exilic theological structure. It may have appeared in a simpler form as early as the reign of Hezekiah. Our conclusion concerning the list is that even though it was written as a warning to the people of Judah, it can be used for our enlightenment of the northern kingdom practices since the activity of Israel at its high places would not have differed greatly from those of Judah. In the next chapter we will look at other scriptural sources that may reveal practices of Israel before its destruction, namely the Elijah-Elisha cycles.

NOTES

1. What is the meaning of the word *secretly?* Most of the activities at high places were public. Perhaps some of the practices were performed in private by individuals. We know that some activity took place at night. Was the historian implying that the people knew the activity was wrong so they had to act in secret? Another translation, however, does not use the word *secretly* but reads "the Israelites uttered words."

2. Israel was finally destroyed by an Assyrian invasion that took place in 722 B.C.E. Shalmaneser V started the invasion, and Sargon II completed it.

Samaria was destroyed, and many Israelites were relocated to Mesopotamia, never to return.

3. At one place we are told that Jeroboam built high places, and in other places we are told that the people built high places. This may reveal more than one stage in the development of DH. For example, in an early edition of DH, the responsibility for Yahweh's blessings or lack of blessings rested with the king. In a later edition, the responsibility was put on the people. There are several examples of this, which we will bring to the readers' attention. For one example, in a summary of Israel's sins, the people are cited as responsible for the erection of the bull calves. Jeroboam is not mentioned (2 Kgs 17:16).

4. A passage in Ezekiel seems to include valleys as possible *bamoth.*

Thus says the LORD God to the mountains and the hills, to the
ravines and the valleys: I…will destroy your high places. (Ez 6:3)
In Jeremiah we read,
…they go on building the high place *(bama)* of Topheth, which is
in the valley of the son of Hinnom. (Jer 7:31)

5. Archaeologists have unearthed large stone platforms at various sites, including Dan. The size of the platform at Dan was eighteen by nineteen meters. See the work of A. Biran in *Biblical Archaeology* 37 (1974) and 43 (1980).

6. We use the words *cultic activity* here without the modern negative connotation of the word cultic.

7. In Judges 17 there is a story of a rich rural family that had its own shrine and its own priest, a Levite from Bethlehem.

8. In an Assyrian record of Sennacherib's attack on Jerusalem in 701, Sennacherib brags that he had laid siege to forty-six of his (Hezekiah's) strong cities and walled forts and to countless small villages.

9. The practice of incubation is not described or condemned in the Deuteronomic torah, but there is a law concerning prophets who divine by dreams (Dt 13:1–5). But for the prophets to be punished, they have to use their incubation role to suggest the worship of other gods besides Yahweh. In post-exilic scripture there may be a condemnation of incubation. Read Isaiah 57.

10. Susan Ackerman, in her monograph *Under Every Green Tree: Popular Religion in Sixth-Century Judah* (see For Further Reading), discusses references to incubation rites in literature from Egypt, Assyria, Babylon, Syria, and Greece. In almost every case a king was involved. Consult the section entitled "Dreaming Dreams in Secret Places" (pp. 194–202).

11. Of course, any student familiar with patriarchal traditions, and even

traditions of premonarchic Israel after the so-called patriarchal period, knows that there was legitimate cultic activity of Yahweh's people at multiple sites.

12. It is interesting to note that the condemnation of Israel's cultic activity is severe, but the Deuteronomic circle seems to have made a decision to supply little specific detail concerning the activities condemned. It is the author's belief that the Deuteronomists shared some characteristics of the Puritans of a much later time. The circle may have felt that a detailed description of the cultic activity of the high places would not only have been in bad taste, but it also may have the possibility of putting ideas in the minds of future readers of the scroll.

13. See Ackerman, *Under Every Green Tree*, pp. 188–90.

14. Gale Yee, in *Composition and Tradition in the Book of Hosea*, states that this passage, Hosea 4:11–14, does not contain original words of Hosea. She attributes these words to R2, an editor I refer to as the exilic editor. Notice the fairness expressed on behalf of the daughters. They do not receive the blame while the men are ignored.

I will not punish your daughters when they play the whore...for the men themselves go aside with whores, and sacrifice with temple prostitutes. (4:14)

The exilic editor forgets for the moment (or chooses to forget) that Hosea was not concerned with the Jerusalem temple but with political decisions made in Samaria.

15. The author of Deuteronomy believes (or wants his reader to believe) that the Israelites came into the land and displaced Canaanites who carried on abhorrent practices related to divination. He may not have been aware that this never happened and that the original Israelites were in fact Canaanites.

16. This law is not repeated in the Deuteronomic torah of Deuteronomy 12–26.

17. No king of Israel was accused of child sacrifice, and no location was cited as a location for child sacrifice in the northern kingdom. Since the only kings cited for child sacrifice were Judean and the place the topheth of the valley of Benhinnom, is it possible that there was no child sacrifice in Israel (the northern kingdom) and the historian included the practice in the list of Israel's sins as a warning to his Judean (Jerusalemite) audience? A vague passage in Hosea mentions "they who sacrifice people," but Gale Yee and others identify the passage as exilic. See Yee's *Composition and Tradition in the Book of Hosea*, p. 249.

14

Elijah, Elisha, and Israel in the Ninth Century

We must remember that the biblical history we are dependent on was produced by a Jerusalemite circle of Levitical priests and scribes that traced its heritage and the origin of its values to the northern Israelite areas of Shechem and Shiloh.[1] We have noted in our study of the Deuteronomic history that the circle that produced the history kept a very low profile. One of the reasons for this was that their ancestors at Shechem, with whom they continued to identify and whose values they perpetuated during the reign of Josiah (640–609), had promoted and approved the break with the house of David after Solomon's death and had played a role in the selection of Jeroboam as the first king of Israel.

Of the political activity of Jeroboam we know very little. Jeroboam became more valuable to the historian as a symbol of rebellion against Yahweh and one of the primary causes of Israel's ultimate destruction.[2]

Following the secession of Israel from the house of David, the northern clans were in no mood to support another strong, oppressive centralized government like that of Solomon's. We have no way of knowing what ambitions the house of Jeroboam had. His dynasty lasted for less than twenty-three years when Baasha assassinated Jeroboam's son Nadab and put a bloody end to the dynasty of Jeroboam (922–900). Because of an unstable monarchy for the first fifty-six years of Israel's existence (three dynasties), there was little opportunity for systematic, administrative exploitation of the rural population. Israel was constantly engaged in on-again, off-again wars with Judah to the south and Syria to the north.

Stability came to the monarchy when Omri became king in 884 B.C.E.[3] Although the Deuteronomic historian gives us almost no information about Omri's reign, we have reason to believe that he "was a very able ruler who had a clear understanding of the political scene...."[4] Israel had lost territory to Aram-Damascus, on both sides of the Jordan[5] and Omri needed an ally. He found this ally in Tyre and sealed a treaty with the Phoenicians that led to his son Ahab's marriage with Jezebel, the daughter of Tyre's king, Ittobaal.

With the reign of Omri, the continual warfare between Israel and Judah came to an end, and Omri, with the support of the army of which he was the commander, was able to subdue Moab as a vassal nation.

> ...King Mesha of Moab...used to deliver to the king of Israel one hundred thousand lambs, and the wool of one hundred thousand rams. (2 Kgs 3:4)

Omri was a military man, and he found the location of Tirzah, enclosed by hills on three sides, unsuitable as a capital for Israel. He acquired the hill of Shemer by purchase, a beautiful location with a view of the surrounding territory and a view of the Mediterranean to the west. Like Jerusalem, Samaria did not have an ancient Yahweh tradition. Omri envisioned a capital for Israel that would surpass Jerusalem in the south.

But you do not construct a magnificent city like Samaria from scratch without a large source of slave labor. Omri, with the support of the army, began to replicate the policies of Solomon and initiated practices that would result in the systematic exploitation of the large rural population of Israel. Omri envisioned a luxurious urban center engaging in international trade through the ports of his ally Phoenicia and the use of the nearby north-south trade route from Egypt to Mesopotamia.

To produce most of the items of international trade and to provide a large source of food and supplies for the urban population that would surround the growing monarchy, Samaria had to control the rural areas adjacent to the capital, along with additional rural areas scattered throughout Israel. Omri died six years after beginning the construction of Samaria. Its building was continued by his son Ahab and subsequent kings of Israel. As the years passed, the gap between the urban rich and the rural poor continued to grow.

It had been because of the burdens placed on the people by Solomon that the Israelites of the north had broken away from the house of David following Solomon's death. We have earlier stated, in our discussion of Solomon's reign, that in times of oppression in Israel, the popularity of Yahweh grew in rural areas as a god of deliverance who would fight for the poor and lower classes of society. We are not surprised then that during the dynasty of Omri voices were raised by champions of Yahweh who would become heroes among segments of the population. We will briefly examine the traditions of Elijah and Elisha to see what they can teach us about religion in the ninth century.

Elijah and Elisha

The Elijah and Elisha cycles are found in the canonical bible from 1 Kings 17 to 2 Kings 13, embedded with other stories of the north. Kings of Israel who are mentioned include Ahab, Ahaziah, and Jehu. Rulers of Judah mentioned include Jehoshaphat, Jehoram, Athaliah, and Joash. Enclosed in the Elijah and Elisha cycles are details concerning Ahab and Jehu. This detail is not characteristic of the Josianic historian's treatment of the northern kings, as can be noticed in the lack of detail in his treatment of Jeroboam I, Omri, and Jeroboam II.

Several factors in the Elijah and Elisha cycles indicate that the viewpoint of the authors differs from the viewpoint of the Josianic historian. (a) In the stories of Elijah and Elisha, these holy men (later called prophets) operate as if Israel had a future. Elsewhere in the Deuteronomic history Israel is condemned from the start because of the sins of Jeroboam. (b) When Elijah meets Yahweh at Horeb, one of his complaints is that the Israelites have "thrown down your altars" (1 Kgs 19:14). One of the basic tenets of DH, however, is that Yahweh forbids all altars except the one at the place he has chosen for his name to dwell (Dt 12). In the Josianic edition of DH, Josiah's reforms include the destruction of the altars, an act that Elijah mourned. (c) In the Elijah stories and the Elisha stories there is no condemnation of the erection of the calf at Bethel and no condemnation of the high places. These two condemnations are trademarks of the Deuteronomic historian. (d) With the inclusion of the Elisha stories, problems are created with the chronology of the Josianic historian. These problems are cleared up when the Elisha stories are removed from DH.[6] (e) The narrator of the Elisha stories does not always know who the king of Israel is and refers to him frequently as "the king of Israel" (2 Kgs 5:5, 7, 8).

Many scholars have concluded that the Elijah and Elisha cycles were not part of the Josianic edition of the Deuteronomic history.[7] These cycles were added to DH during or after the period of exile (587–539). The cycles as they now appear in the canonical bible contain signs of Deuteronomistic editing that must be taken into consideration if we are to determine which portions date to the ninth century. The portions of the material that have a northern origin may give us some insight into the religious practices of Israel in the ninth century.

Deuteronomistic Characteristics

(a) The most dramatic story of Elijah is the confrontation with the priests of the Tyrian Baal on Mount Carmel. We notice some similarities between this story and incidents in the book of Joshua. Like Joshua, Elijah addresses *the people,* as if all of Israel could be gathered within the sound of his voice. This idealistic concept of the people is characteristic of the exilic (587–539) Deuteronomistic editor.[8] (b) The people are challenged with a choice between Yahweh and other gods. Joshua tells the people to choose between Yahweh or the gods of the Amorites.

> Choose this day whom you will serve. (Jos 24:15–16)

Elijah says to *the people* on Mount Carmel,

> How long will you go limping with two different opinions? If the LORD is god, follow him; but if Baal, then follow him. (1 Kgs 18:21)

Presenting the people with a choice is a Deuteronomistic characteristic. (c) Both Joshua and Elijah use twelve stones to represent the twelve tribes of Israel (Jos 4:1–9, 1 Kgs 18:31–32).[9] (d) Both Elijah and Joshua part the waters of the Jordan River (2 Kgs 2:8–14, Jos 3). (e) It should also be noted that when Elijah faces King Ahab following the stealing of Naboth's vineyard (1 Kgs 21), Elijah is not the holy man miracle worker but a Deuteronomic prophet concerned with law and justice.

**DEUTERONOMISTIC CHARACTERISTICS
IN THE ELIJAH CYCLE**

CHART 11

1. Both Joshua and Elijah address *all Israel,* as if the entire nation could be gathered in one location (Jos 24, 1 Kgs 18:19).
2. Both Joshua and Elijah challenge the people to choose between Yahweh and other gods.
3. Both use twelve stones to represent the twelve tribes of Israel (Jos 4:1–9, 1 Kgs 18:31–32).
4. Both part the waters of the Jordan (Jos 3, 2 Kgs 2:8–14).
5. When Elijah faces Ahab in the vineyard of Naboth, he is not a holy man miracle worker but a Deuteronomistic prophet concerned with law and justice (1 Kgs 21).

Our purpose in pointing out the above characteristics of the canonical Elijah stories is to remind ourselves that only a portion of the Elijah-Elisha cycles dates to the ninth century. The Elijah-Elisha cycles became part of DH during or after the exile but not before important Deuteronomistic editing.

Regional Baals

There has been a dispute among scholars concerning the identification of the Baal of Mount Carmel challenged by Elijah.[10] This dispute reminds us that the word *Baal* is not only the name of a god of fertility and a storm god in Syrian mythology but also a *title* of local fertility gods worshiped in the territory of Israel for centuries. In 1 Kings 18:18 Elijah is quoted as saying,

> ...you have forsaken the commandments of the LORD and followed the Baals.[11]

When we say there were regional Baals, we have to remind ourselves that we are not speaking of objective reality but of regional differences in the perception of Baal, his nature and role, in various regions of Israel. Differing perspectives must be assumed considering the fact that the land occupied by Israel had a severely fragmented topography and there was little and infrequent communication between regions. That the farmers of Israel would have recognized the need for Baal worship in the ninth century was natural. The worship of a Baal was part of the Canaanite heritage. The bible history would lead us to believe that recognition of Baal by the farmers of Israel was a grievous falling away from a pure form of Yahweh worship that had characterized a former age. This was an idealization of Israel's past. We must continue to remember that it is necessary to distinguish between Israel of the bible and Israel that produced the bible. The time when historical Israel would be challenged to embrace Yahweh and reject all other gods was still in Israel's future.

Jehu

During the reign of the house of Omri, Yahweh grew in importance in some of the rural areas and changed the theology of important centers of worship, high places controlled by strong priesthoods who, in some cases, opposed the practices of the reigning king. As we have suggested, Yahweh was perceived as a god for the underclasses of society.

The entire history of the northern kingdom was characterized by gross acts of widespread violence. Many individuals seized the throne by murdering the reigning king and/or killing the members of the royal family. Individuals who seized the throne by assassination and murder include Baasha, Zimri, Jehu, Shallum, Menahem, and Pekah. It was a common practice in the ancient Near East for a monarch establishing a new dynasty to produce scrolls of legitimation to justify acts of cruelty and violence carried out by the new monarch in seizing the throne.

It is our assumption that during the reign of Ahab, with the rising importance of the Tyrian Baal in Samaria, at least two holy men emerged as champions of Yahweh, Elijah and Elisha. Historically, these two holy persons were not prophets in the Deuteronomistic sense but were itinerant miracle workers

---

SEIZING THE THRONE OF ISRAEL BY ASSASSINATION

CHART 12

Nadab killed by Baasha, 900 B.C.E. (1 Kgs 15:25–31).

Elah killed by Zimri, 876 (1 Kgs 16:8–10).

Joram killed by Jehu, 842 (2 Kgs 9:14–25).

Zechariah killed by Shallum, 752 (2 Kgs 15:8–10).

Shallum killed by Menahem, 752 (2 Kgs 13–14).

Pekahiah killed by Pekah, 741 (2 Kgs 15:23–25).

---

and oracle givers. The transformation of Elijah and Elisha into prophets *(nabiim)* would take place centuries later in the scrolls of the Deuteronomistic circle.

There may be some historical truth to the actions of Jehu based on his taking advantage of an anti-Baal, pro-Yahweh movement in rural areas of Israel during the ninth century. The scribes who were given the task of legitimizing Jehu wisely pictured Elijah and Elisha as supporters of Jehu (1 Kgs 19:15–18, 2 Kgs 9:1–13) and Jehu as a champion of the people's god, Yahweh. In the ninth-century legitimization document produced by the scribes of Jehu's court, Jehu is quoted as declaring himself a zealot for Yahweh in fulfillment of Elijah's words:

> "Come with me [Jehu] and see my zeal for Yahweh." When Jehu came to Samaria, he killed all who were left to Ahab in Samaria, until he had wiped them out, according to the word of the LORD that he [Yahweh] spoke to Elijah. (2 Kgs 10:16–17)

The Josianic historian in presenting the history of the northern kingdom did not record detail and information of any significance for the reigns of important kings such as Jeroboam and Omri. For this reason many scholars have concluded that the detail supplied for us concerning the reigns of Ahab and Jehu may not have been part of the Josianic edition of DH but, like the Elijah and Elisha cycles, became part of DH during or after the exile.

In DH as we have received it, it is stated that during the reign of Jehu,

> ...the LORD began to trim off parts of Israel. (2 Kgs 10:32)

Although not mentioned in the bible, most scholars believe that Jehu was able to seize the throne of Israel because he made a contract to become a vassal of Assyria, which was involved in a massive effort to control the entire Palestine-Syria area. Shalmaneser III (858–824) bragged in the record of his military activity of reaching the Mediterranean and produced the magnificent "black obelisk," picturing in one of its registers *Jehu, son of Omri,* as a vassal king on his knees offering tribute to Shalmaneser.[12]

Conclusions

It is probable that the Elijah and Elisha cycles, including details concerning the reigns of Ahab and Jehu, were not part of the earliest (Josianic) edition of the Deuteronomic history. The material as we now have it is heavily edited but at its core is some valuable insight into ninth-century Israel.

(a) Ahab did build a temple for Baal in Samaria for his Phoenician wife Jezebel and continued building projects in Israel that demanded slave labor, reproducing the abuses of Solomon in nonurban areas. Solomon's practices had led to the revolt of the northern clans from the house of David.

(b) Yahweh's importance as a god of deliverance increased among the rural clans (at high places nevertheless).

(c) Saints, local heroes, or holy persons appeared who spoke out for Yahweh. Behind the Elijah and Elisha stories were two prominent historical persons who were promoters of Yahweh.

(d) The tone of the Elijah-Elisha stories differs from DH in that they seem to promote Israel's future as redeemable, while in DH passages Israel is condemned from the start because of Jeroboam's acts.

(e) Elijah's mourning over the neglect and destruction of Yahweh's altars is inconsistent with the theology of DH.

(f) There is no condemnation of high places or the bull calf of Bethel by Elijah or Elisha.

(g) The earliest written document telling of Elijah and Elisha could have been produced by the court of Jehu to legitimate the violent seizing of the throne by Jehu, who declared himself a Yahwist to gain support of the rural clans.

In the next chapter we will discuss the reign of a son of the house of Jehu, Jeroboam II. During his reign Samaria received a visit from an angry Judean social critic by the name of Amos of Tekoa.

NOTES

1. Many scholars believe that Israelite cult activity was severely diminished at Shiloh following its destruction by the Philistines in 1050 B.C.E. It is possible that following the secession of the northern clans, the strong Yahweh sect at Shechem expanded its activity to some extent in the Shiloh area, ten miles to the south of Shechem.

2. Jeroboam did three things that made him the enemy of the Levitical priests of Shechem. First, he moved his capital from Shechem to Penuel (and later to Tirzah); second, he established Bethel and Dan as the official shrines of the new nation; and third, he appointed priests for the official shrines who were not Levites.

3. The *NJBC* states that Omri became king of Israel in 876 (p. 1233). The date we are using, 884, is from a monograph, *Studies in the Chronology of the Divided Monarchy*, by W. H. Barnes (p. 153).

4. Ahlstrom, *The History of Ancient Palestine*, p. 571.

5. Damascus had invaded Galilee and had gained control of the major trade route as it passed through northern Transjordan. See Ahlstrom, *Ancient Palestine*, pp. 570–71.

6. See McKenzie's *The Trouble with Kings*, pp. 97–98.

7. McKenzie, in his recent study cited above, supplies many references to scholarly works that support the belief that the Elisha cycle and parts of the Elijah cycle were exilic or postexilic additions to DH, including works by J. M. Miller, H. J. Stipp, and J. van Seters.

8. For example, the exilic Deuteronomistic editor, sometimes called DTR2, states that *the people* erected the golden calves at Bethel and Dan rather than Jeroboam in 2 Kings 17:16:

And they [the people] forsook the commandments of the LORD their God, and *made for themselves* molten images of two calves.

9. The question may be raised, Why would Elijah, a northern prophet, be interested at all in the traditional twelve tribes of Israel?

10. For example, see *Religion and Culture in Ancient Israel* by J. Andrew Dearman (1992), pp. 74–78.

11. In 2 Chronicles we are told that in the presence of Josiah, "they pulled down the altars of the Baals."

12. See *The Ancient Near East: An Anthology of Texts and Pictures,* Vol. 1, (1973), plate 100a.

15

Amos, Hosea, and the Eighth Century

The house of Jehu continued well into the eighth century, and its most important king was Jehu's grandson, Jeroboam II. The fact that his father Joash (801–786) named him Jeroboam is an indication that Jeroboam I was remembered and respected in Israel. Jeroboam II reigned for forty years (786–746). It is especially interesting to note that the historian reports that

> ...the LORD [Yahweh] saved them [Israel] by the hand of Jeroboam the son of Joash. (2 Kgs 14:27)

Because of problems in the Far East that temporarily distracted Assyria[1] and interrupted Assyria's constant domination of the Palestine-Syria area, Jeroboam II was able to restore territory lost to Israel. After early military victories, Samaria began to experience unprecedented prosperity. Commerce became active, business flourished, and international trade and building activity increased. In the ancient Near East people in royal capital cities, like Samaria, did not get rich by working hard. They lived lives of luxury and comfort by structuring society in such as way as to live off the labor of the rural masses. Urban dwellers did not grow their own food, build capital palaces or grand houses, or fight their own battles. By manipulating the rural farmers of Israel, the population of Samaria grew richer and the masses grew poorer. Ancient Israelite land rights were suspended, slavery for debt became common, and justice was manipulated in favor of the rich. Those who grew the food for urban dwellers did not eat as well as the idle rich, and there was a demand for crops and produce for the use of international trade rather than for the needs of rural family survival. The ancient institutions of agricultural Israel that had made it possible for Israel to survive before the coming of the monarchy without a centralized government were destroyed. In premonarchical Israel the intergenerational family *(beth-av)* had been the central institution of society, the institution all other institutions encircled and protected. By the eighth century this constellation was a memory. By the reign of Jeroboam II, the central institution, the one that had to be preserved at any cost, was the monarchy. It was in response to the suffering of the rural poor that Amos of Tekoa made his appearance.

Amos of Tekoa

While the scroll of Amos contained the oracles of the historical Amos, most scholars easily recognize two editorial levels *in addition to* the words of Amos. The original words of Amos constitute less than 30 percent of the canonical scroll. So the words of Amos dating from the eighth century are found scattered in a liturgical structure created by a scribe of the Deuteronomic circle during the days of Josiah, the late seventh century. Further words were added during the exile.

Since our purpose is to discover what Amos reveals about eighth-century Israel, we have to identify the original oracles. Robert B. Coote, in a discerning and sensitive book on the oracles of Amos, *Amos Among the Prophets,*[2] is able to point out nine characteristics that identify the original oracles of Amos. The serious student is urged to read this book for a convincing understanding of these characteristics. For our purposes, however, it is essential to identify only the following about the original oracles of Amos: They are earthy, specific, down to earth, and concrete. They address a specific situation at a specific time. Amos did not use abstract general words like "good," "evil," "justice," or "righteousness."[3] So simplistic passages like the following cannot be attributed to Amos:

> Seek good and not evil. (5:14)

More important, the famous passage that begins with the words "I hate, I despise your festivals" and ends with the words

> But let Justice roll down like waters, and righteousness like an everflowing stream (5:21–24)

should not be attributed to Amos either.

For an example of an authentic Amos oracle, we have many choices. Notice the picturesque concreteness of the following.

> ...because you trample on the poor
> and take from them levies of grain
> you have built houses of hewn stone,
> but you shall not live in them;
> you have planted pleasant vineyards,
> but you shall not drink their wine....
> you...who take a bribe, and push aside the needy in the gate.
> (5:11–12)

Here is another example of the concreteness of Amos's oracles.

> As a shepherd rescues from the mouth of the lion two legs, or a
> piece of an ear, so shall the people of Israel who dwell in Samaria
> be rescued, with the corner of a couch and part of a bed. (3:4)

The above passage also contains another important characteristic of Amos's oracles. They are addressed to those who dwell in Samaria. Amos held the decision makers of Samaria responsible for the hardships of the rural poor. The victims of economic injustice are identified as the poor, the needy, and in two places the righteous (2:6 and 5:12).

Amos calls for witnesses to gather on the mountains to see the destruction that will take place on the day of Yahweh. He ends his oracles by declaring that not one oppressor shall escape. (9:1–4)

> And though they go into captivity in front of their enemies, there I
> will command the sword, and it shall kill them. (9:4)

Some have seen no positive side to the message of Amos. He seems to be delivering a message of destruction with no opportunity for change and escape. This is true. When there is an opportunity for change, such as

> Seek me and live....Seek the LORD and live....Seek good and not
> evil that you may live (5:4, 6, 14),

we are not reading the words of Amos, but words provided in the scroll by a scribe of the Deuteronomic circle, a hundred years after the death of Amos. But it is important to remember that although the eighth-century Amos was delivering a proclamation that was irreversible, he was also proclaiming that there was one who did not forget justice.[4] The God of Amos was after all a God of fair treatment, who would not tolerate the abuse of his people. His people were the oppressed and powerless.

The Marzeah

In recent decades scholars have recognized references to the *marzeah* banquet in the oracles of Amos.[5] The *marzeah* was an ancient Canaanite practice in which only the wealthy members of society could participate. It involved the holding of a sumptuous feast in a special building, called the *beth marzeah*, set apart for the occasion. The *marzeah* building was jointly owned by those entitled to participate in the feast. The feast would last for several days and was organized under the patronage of a god. In some of the literature of the ancient Near East, the feast was associated with mourning the death of a member of the *marzeah* society.

During the *marzeah* feast it was common for participants to recline on couches, eat the meat of stall-fed animals, anoint themselves with expensive oils, and drink large quantities of wine from gold and silver bowls. Over-indulgence was the rule of the day. Although the etymology of the word *marzeah* is uncertain, Philip King sees in the following words of Amos a direct reference to the *marzeah* banquet:[6]

> Woe to those who lie on beds of ivory,
> and lounge on their couches,
> and eat lambs from the flock,
>   and calves from the stall....
> who drink wine from bowls and anoint themselves
> with the finest of oils....
> the revelry [*marzeah*] of the loungers shall pass
> away. (6:4–7)

What Do Amos's Oracles Tell Us About Religion?

The eighth-century oracles of Amos give us a vital and extremely important picture of social imbalance in eighth-century Israel. He directs his words of condemnation against the decision makers of Samaria, for whom there will be no escape. But Amos says nothing about the religious practices of the time. He does not mention idolatry, high places, sacrifices, Bethel, mediums, or human sacrifice. His criticism of the *marzeah* is based on the luxurious lifestyle of the participants and not the fact that the feasts were frequently held in the name of a patronage god, Baal, El, Asherah, and sometimes even Yahweh.[7] He despises the *marzeah* because it is an institution of the rich and displays con-spicuous consumption.

When particular religious practices are condemned in the scroll of Amos, we can attribute these passages to a seventh-century scribe of Judah, a member of the Deuteronomic circle.[8] This includes all passages that condemn the practices of the popular shrine at Bethel, to support the destruction of Bethel by King Josiah.

Hosea

Hosea is recognized as a prophet of the northern kingdom of Israel. Like the scroll of Amos, the scroll of Hosea contains his authentic oracles, embedded in a liturgical and theological structure provided by at least two editors who lived long after the death of Hosea. Gale Yee, in her book *Composition and Tradition in the Book of Hosea,* identifies the hands of three authors/editors in the canonical book of Hosea in addition to Hosea himself.

The original oracles of Hosea, like the original oracles of Amos, were directed to the decision makers of Samaria.

> Hear this, O priests!
> Give heed, O house of Israel
> Hearken, O house of the king!
> For judgement pertains to you. (Hos 5:1–2)

An examination of the oracles of Hosea reveals to us that the sin of Samaria was the making of treaties with Egypt against Assyria and with Assyria against Egypt. The oracles of Hosea are filled with pain and anger. Following the death of Jeroboam II, Hosea saw Israel's leaders making the wrong decisions and leading the people to economic and military destruction. Instead of calling on Yahweh, Israel trusted in military strength for deliverance, either its own or the military strength of others. In running to these foreign powers, Israel acted like a harlot.

> O Ephraim, you have played the harlot. (5:3)

> Ephraim is like a dove, silly and without sense,
> calling to Egypt, going to Assyria. (7:11)

> For they have gone up to Assyria, a wild ass
> wandering alone;
> Ephraim has hired lovers.
> Though they have hired allies among the nations,
> I will soon gather them up. (8:8–10)

Like Isaiah of Jerusalem, Hosea was critical of foreign alliances in place of complete trust in Yahweh as a deliverer of Israel. Hosea was a political critic.

When the oracles of Hosea were emended by a Josianic scribe (probably between 621 and 609 B.C.E.), the audience was changed, and the sin addressed was also changed. Writing at a time when Israel (the northern kingdom) as a nation-state no longer existed, the new audience consisted of the people of Judah, and the sin was now cultic impurity, worshiping gods besides Yahweh, and doing things that were an abomination to Yahweh as revealed in the Deuteronomic torah (Dt 12–26).

Who Preserved the Words of Amos and Hosea?

The original words of Amos reveal Amos as a severe social critic. As we have stated he had nothing to say about the cultic practices of high places. Hosea was a political critic, condemning Israel (Samaria) by the use of harsh metaphors. Among other things Hosea called Israel/Ephraim a harlot, a sick person, a cake not turned, a silly dove, a useless vessel, and a wild ass.[9] Neither Amos nor Hosea had much to say that would reveal the religious practices of Samaria or Israel. Criticism of cultic practices was added to both books a century later by the scribes of the Deuteronomic circle. It is this fact that informs us of the group that preserved the oracles of Amos and Hosea.

It is our conclusion that the personnel of a strong Yahweh, anti-Samaria, cult center at Shechem, between the mountains of Gerazim and Ebal, preserved the oracles of both Amos and Hosea. This cult center provided the foundation for the seventh-century theology of the priests and scribes that produced the book of Deuteronomy (in several stages), the Deuteronomic and Deuteronomistic history, and the updated versions of the eighth-century prophets.

When the northern tribes seceded from the house of David following the death of Solomon, it was to Shechem that Solomon's son Rehoboam had to go to negotiate for his throne. Following the rejection of Rehoboam and the coronation of Jeroboam as the first king of Israel, the new nation-state, we are informed that Jeroboam moved from Shechem to Penuel and from there to Tirzah. These moves were for the purpose of diminishing the domination of the Levitical priests of Shechem. When the two border shrines were selected, Bethel and Dan, we are informed that Jeroboam

...appointed priests from among all the people, who were not Levites. (1 Kgs 12:31)

The Levitical descendants of the Shechem shrine provided the first priesthood that recognized the importance of written scrolls as a revelation of Yahweh, and the creation of scrolls containing the words of Amos and Hosea may have been early examples of the many scrolls that would later compose the Hebrew bible. Was the Shechem site an early example of a Yahweh-only shrine? From the evidence available to us, we cannot say with certainty that this was true in the eighth century. We can safely assume that this anti-Samaria cult site was a strong Yahweh center. Also, we can safely say that the descendants of this group of priests and scribes would produce the strong Yahweh-only theologians of the Josianic reign (640–609 B.C.E.) known to scholars as the Deuteronomic circle.[10]

NOTES

1. The kingdom of Urartu gained power and kept Assyria occupied and out of the Syria-Palestine area from 810 to 743.

2. Robert Coote's book, *Amos Among the Prophets,* was published by Fortress Press in 1981.

3. For a popular treatment of Amos and his oracles, see my Paulist Press book *Prophet of Justice*, 1989.

4. Robert Coote, *Amos Among the Prophets*, p. 41.

5. For two examples see Philip J. King's book *Amos, Hosea, Micah— An Archaeological Commentary* (Westminster Press, 1988), pp. 137–61; and Susan Ackerman's book *Under Every Green Tree* (Scholars Press, 1992), pp. 71–79.

6. King, *Amos, Hosea, Micah,* p. 137.

7. See Ackerman, *Under Every Green Tree*, p. 79, and Mark S. Smith, *Early History of God*, p. 131.

8. Amos may have quoted Yahweh as saying, "I will turn your feasts into mourning and all your songs into lamentation" (8:10). In many cultures festivals are tied to religious traditions, but the basis for the condemnation of Yahweh with these words was the cruel exploitation of the masses, not the practices of public religion.

9. The metaphors listed can be found as follows: a harlot (2:4b), a sick person (5:13), a cake not turned (7:8), a silly dove (7:11), a useless vessel (8:8), a wild ass (8:9). For further detail concerning the metaphors from the book of Hosea consult the author's book *Prophet of Love: Understanding the Book of Hosea* (Paulist Press, 1991).

10. For a more detailed discussion of the connection between Shechem and the Deuteronomic circle, see my book *Obsession with Justice: The Story of the Deuteronomists* (Paulist Press, 1994), pp. 25–36. Of particular note is the place that Shechem plays in Deuteronomy and Joshua, both products of the Deuteronomists. In both books the legendary twelve tribes gather on the two mountains that surround the Shechem area after entering the land, six tribes on each mountain, to read (hear) portions of the torah.

16

The Last Days of the Northern Kingdom

The reign of Jeroboam II lasted for forty years frequently characterized by prosperity in Samaria and peace for Israel. Following the death of Jeroboam II (746), ambitious people close to the center of power decided that they had had enough of a good thing, and Israel entered a final period in her history, characterized by chaos and murder in the royal court. In the twelve-year period following the death of Jeroboam, three of the four kings took the throne by murdering their predecessors. The house of Jehu (of which Jeroboam II was a son) came to an end when a son of Jeroboam, Zechariah, was assassinated by Shallum after reigning for only six months.

> Shallum...conspired against him [Zechariah], and struck him down at Ibleam, and killed him, and reigned in his stead. (2 Kgs 15:10)

Shallum himself had an even shorter reign. He was killed by Menahem after one month (745).

In summary, following the death of Jeroboam II, six kings reigned in Israel. Hoshea (732–722), an on-again, off-again vassal of Assyria, was the final king when Samaria was destroyed in 722 B.C.E. The last days of the northern kingdom reveal tragic times for Israel, and as you read the chronicle of mayhem and bloodshed, you get the clear impression that Yahweh was unknown to the so-called powerful of Samaria. Admittedly our main source of information is DH. But there is not a hint in the account of the last twenty-four years of any acknowledgement of Yahweh's role in the history of the nation by any king, prince, or significant political leader.

Bethel and Dan

There is a surprising lack of detail provided in DH concerning Bethel and Dan after their establishment by Jeroboam as the national shrines of Israel. On the basis of a repeated formulaic statement criticizing the individual kings of Israel for not departing from the sins of Jeroboam, the son of Nebat, most scholars have assumed that Dan and Bethel continued to be the official shrines of the nation. If this was the case, why are there so few references to Dan and Bethel in the history?

The shrine at Dan may never have gotten off the ground. Shortly after the death of Jeroboam, his dynasty expired, and during the reign of Baasha (900–877) we are told that Benhadad of Damascus captured Dan and all the land of Naphtali (1 Kgs 15:20). Benhadad not only captured Dan but also ravished the land west of the Lake of Gennesaret. The historian does not mention that Dan was the national shrine of Israel in the north.[1]

During the Elijah-Elisha cycle Bethel is mentioned in a neutral tone with no hint that it was the national shrine, home of the infamous bull calf.

> So they [Elijah and Elisha] went down to Bethel. The company of the prophets who were in Bethel came out to Elisha, and said to him, "Do you know that today the LORD will take your master away from you?" And he said, "Yes I know, keep silent." (2 Kgs 2:3)

There is no condemnatory remark concerning Bethel here.[2]

There is not one reference in DH of the involvement of any king of Israel in or with Bethel after the death of Jeroboam. There is one incident of interest, however, found in the canonical book of Amos. This is the third-person account of the encounter of Amos with Amaziah, a priest of Bethel. In this encounter Amaziah reports to Jeroboam II concerning Amos's oracles of doom and reports that the land is not able to bear all his words. Amaziah later says to Amos,

> O seer, go flee away to the land of Judah, earn your bread there, and prophesy there; but never again prophesy at Bethel, for it is the king's sanctuary, and it is a temple of the kingdom. (Am 7:12–13)

There is no way to document the historicity of this incident, and it is out of character for Amos to deliver an oracle against an individual, as he subsequently does (v. 17) against Amaziah. This story included in the scroll of Amos would serve well to further discredit Bethel and justify its destruction during the reign of Josiah. There is an interesting puzzle here, however. Amos replies to Amaziah, when Amaziah commands him to leave Bethel and return to Judah,

I am no prophet [*nabi*], nor a prophet's son. (7:14).

There are two interesting questions. (1) Amaziah did not call Amos a *nabi*, he called him a seer *(hozeh)*. (2) If a scribe of the Deuteronomic circle inserted this story in the text, why did he report that Amos denied being a *nabi*, the Deuteronomists' favorite word for "prophet"? For example, in an earlier place in the scroll of Amos the Deuteronomists inserted this theological statement (3:7).

> Surely the LORD God does nothing, without revealing his secret to
> his servants the prophets [*nabiim*].

We will answer the questions above in chapter 23 of this book, "The Invention of the Prophetic Class," where we will suggest that Amos did not become a prophet, *nabi,* until more than a century after his death.

Were Bethel and Dan Really the Two National Shrines?

What we are saying about Dan and Bethel is that even though Jeroboam intended that Dan and Bethel should be the official high places of Israel, his plans may have faltered with the fall of his dynasty. Dan was destroyed during the reign of Baasha (900–877), and there is no report of any king of Israel visiting or being involved in the so-called national shrine of Bethel. It is our suggestion that Bethel flourished as a high place under the care of a non-Levitical priesthood and as such was in competition with the Levitical priesthood of Shechem. Bethel may have been a strong cult center with a view of Yahweh worship that ran counter to the view of Yahweh espoused by the Shechem circle, where Yahweh was emerging as a god of law, cultic purity, and unity. During the reign of Jeroboam I, Bethel, already a well-established Canaanite cult center, picked up the title as a royal shrine, but this title may have been largely ignored by the subsequent kings of Israel.[3]

The historian had little interest in relating the details of the reigns of the kings of Israel. We see this in his description of the reigns of Baasha, Omri, and Jeroboam II. But whether a king reigned for forty years or six months, the historian would write an assessment similar to this.

> He did not depart from the sins of Jeroboam son of Nebat, which
> he caused Israel to sin.

By doing this he created a chronological unity for Israel that did not exist. Israel had nine dynasties, the borders kept changing, and Israel got smaller and smaller until the last king, Hoshea, reigned over part of one tribe, Ephraim. In Hosea's oracles he referred to Israel as Ephraim. Israel lacked political and religious unity. Israel was neither monotheistic nor monolatrous. But the appearance of unity, created by the Josianic version of Joshua and bolstered by other parts of DH, was important to the historian, who, during the reign of Josiah (640–609), had a vision that involved the acquisition of Samarina, the Assyrian province that occupied the territory north of Judah.

Shalmaneser V started the final chapter of Israel, and Sargon II finished it with the destruction of Samaria and the deportation of a great part of the population.

> The people of Israel continued in all the sins that Jeroboam committed; they did not depart from them until the LORD removed Israel out of his sight....So Israel was exiled from their own land to Assyria until this day. (2 Kgs 17:22–23)

NOTES

1. Later, during the reign of Jehu (842–815), there is a remark about Jehu not removing the bull calves of *Dan* and Bethel (2 Kgs 10:29). It is obviously a gloss.

2. It is probable that the Elijah-Elisha cycle, which was not written by the Josianic historian, was not part of the original history, the Josianic edition. With the Elijah-Elisha cycle removed, the theological and political purpose of the Josianic edition is much clearer.

3. Because Bethel was such a *natural* high place, with a favorable site and a long tradition, it survived as a shrine following the destruction of Samaria by the Assyrians. We are told that the Assyrians sent an Israelite priest of Yahweh back from exile to Bethel to teach the people how to worship properly at Bethel (2 Kgs 17:27–28). We will have more to say about Bethel after the destruction of Israel when we discuss the problem of Bethel during the reign of Josiah.

Part IV
SHECHEMITE PRIESTS
IN JUDAH
(922–586 B.C.E.)

17

Judah After Secession

In part III we searched the canonical version of the Deuteronomistic history (the final version that appears in our bibles) to see what is revealed about the practice of religion in the northern kingdom, Israel. We were constantly aware that there are several layers of authorship in DH and that from the earliest author (preexilic) through to the last editor (postexilic), a theological interpretation of the past was more important than historical fact. We paid attention to the way the historians/authors used their sources, sometimes intentionally and sometimes unintentionally revealing facts about religious practices in the northern kingdom.

We now continue our review of DH, this time turning our attention to the nation-state of Judah in the south, a nation that survived after the destruction of Israel (722) for 135 years.

One of the chief differences between Judah and Israel was the role of the capital city of Judah, Jerusalem. There is no doubt that Jerusalem was the center of official state religious activity in Judah. In our review of Israel, although we were told that the official shrines were Dan in the north and Bethel in the south, we noticed some weaknesses of this view. First of all, we suggested that Dan as a national shrine may never have gotten off the ground. There is no doubt that Dan was an ancient Canaanite cultic center, and we can believe that Jeroboam may have designated Dan as the northern border shrine of Israel, but Dan is ignored in DH except for a few references, one of which tells us about the capture of the territory of Dan by Benhadad of Damascus during the reign of Baasha (900–877).

> Benhadad...conquered Ijon, Dan, Abelbethmaacah, and all Chinnerith, with the land of Naphtali. (1 Kgs 15:20)

Not only is Dan ignored in DH, but after the death of Jeroboam (901), there is hardly any mention of Bethel, *apart from the condemnatory stereotypical statements about each king continuing in the sins of Jeroboam.* After the death of Jeroboam, there is not one reference of a king of Israel visiting or interacting with Bethel in DH.[1]

As we review the accounts of the reigns of the kings in Judah, we will be aware of something we noted in our review of the north—that the primary purpose of the historian was not to record historical facts. We notice this when we look at the accounts of the reigns of Uzziah and Manasseh. Uzziah (Azariah) reigned for fifty-two years, and Manasseh for fifty-five years, and the facts of their reigns supplied for us could be written on an index card.

The Kings of Judah after Secession of the North

Israel survived for two hundred years during which time Judah had twelve rulers.[2]

RULERS OF JUDAH AFTER SECESSION UNTIL 722 CHART 13	
Rehoboam	922–915
Abijam (Abijah)	915–913
Asa	913–873
Jehoshaphat	873–849
Joram (Jehoram)	849–842
Ahaziah	842
Queen Athaliah	842–837
Joash (Jehoash)	837–800
Amaziah	800–783
Uzziah (Azariah)	783–742
Jotham	742–735
Ahaz (Jehoahaz)	735–715

We note that in the reporting formula of each new reign the name of the king's mother is given.[3] Here are two examples.

> Rehoboam was forty-one years old when he began to reign, and he reigned seventeen years in Jerusalem....His mother's name was Naamah the Ammonite. (1 Kgs 14:21)
>
> Now in the eighteenth year of king Jeroboam [of Israel]...Abijam began to reign over Judah. He reigned for three years in Jerusalem. His mother's name was Maacah daughter of Abishalom. (1 Kgs 15:2)

Why was the name of the mother included? Many believe that there was an official role for the king's mother (queen mother) in Judah that was not observed in Israel.[4] Supporting this view is a report that King Asa (913–873) removed his mother from her position as queen mother.

> He [Asa] also removed his mother Maacah from being queen mother, because she had made an abominable image for Asherah. Asa cut down her image, and burned it at the Wadi Kidron. (1 Kgs 15:13)

The fact that Asa cut down the image and burned it indicates that the Asherah image was made of wood.

The historian (or a later editor) included in the description of Rehoboam's reign a statement about religious practices in Judah.

> For they [the Judahites] also built for themselves high places, pillars and sacred poles on every high hill and under every green tree. (1 Kgs 14:23)

The author is reminding the reader that just because there is a national temple in Jerusalem, that doesn't mean that multiple shrines were any less a problem in Judah than in Israel.

After the secession of the northern tribes, things continued to deteriorate for Rehoboam of Judah (922–915). King Shishak of Egypt invaded Judah and came against Jerusalem. The Philistines regained power, and shortly thereafter the Moabites, Ammonites, and Aramaeans shook off the domination of Jerusalem.

> King Shishak...took away the treasures of the house of the LORD. (1 Kgs 14:25–26)

Judah was always differentiated from Israel (the north) because of the existence of the temple adjacent to the palace. Israel had nothing compared to the temple of Solomon, although the Omri city of Samaria was a magnificent city by ancient standards. The temple legitimated the monarchy and the dynasty of the house of David.

What is interesting about the Shishak invasion is the reference to the treasures of the house of the LORD. As we make our way through the reigns of the kings of Judah, we will find that repeatedly the house of the LORD is stripped of its gold, silver, and other treasures. For different reasons this happens during the reigns of Rehoboam, Asa, Amaziah, Ahaz, and Hezekiah. This raises a question about the ornateness of the temple and the source for the *renewal* of the house's gold, silver, and other treasures. We do know that storerooms encircled the temple on three sides. The store consisted of religious objects, precious gifts from other nations and perhaps individuals, tribute collected from the people as taxes, and booty obtained from defeated enemies. Perhaps there were also items gathered as a result of international trade.

Male Temple Prostitutes in the Land?

In the short description of Rehoboam's reign, we are informed that Judah, like Israel, built many high places with pillars and sacred poles. A practice that was of concern to the historian (or editor) was singled out.

> …there were also male temple prostitutes in the land. (1 Kgs 14:24)

In the New Revised Standard Version of the Old Testament, references to male temple prostitutes are included in the description of the reigns of Asa, Jehoshaphat, and Josiah. We are told that Asa (913–873) put away the male temple prostitutes that were in the land and removed all the idols his ancestors had made. Later we are told that Jehoshaphat son of Asa (873–849) exterminated male temple prostitutes who were left from his father's purge (1 Kgs 22:46).

Many scholars believe that there were no male cultic prostitutes and that the Hebrew phrase refers to non-Yahwistic priests.[5]

What is the significance of the phrase "in the land"? It may mean that non-Yahwistic priests, perhaps promoting the use of idols (or male prostitutes?), were in the temple complex at one time but were banished, only to continue their practice elsewhere in Judah where they were acceptable or at least tolerated. Much later, at the end of the seventh century, as part of the Deuteronomic reforms of Josiah we read:

> He [Josiah] broke down the houses of the male temple prostitutes
> that were in the house of the LORD. (2 Kgs 23:7)

While we cannot solve the above scholarly argument, there is something important to be observed. The indication is that the king of Judah had a role in temple management and a role in the reformation of practices at high places in the land. Although limited in scope, both Asa and Jehoshaphat were involved in reforms. This sets the stage for the ambitious reforms attributed to Hezekiah and later to Josiah.

The Damascus Altar of Ahaz

If we read the Old Testament uncritically, we get the impression that all specifications for the Jerusalem temple complex were of divine origin. Books of the Pentateuch (Exodus, Leviticus, Numbers) give the impression that all measurements of the tabernacle in the wilderness, including detailed instructions for the furniture and other cult items, come straight from Yahweh, and carry over into the age of the monarchy when David is forbidden to build a temple and Solomon is approved.

What we forget is that there was no tabernacle in the wilderness shared by tribes of Jacob. The description of the tabernacle in Exodus 25 to 40 is a projection into the wilderness tradition by the priestly party. The description of the tabernacle was based on the temple of Jerusalem under the guise of a portable sanctuary.[6]

The actual plan for the temple came from other ancient temples of the Near East, the Syrian-Phoenician area in particular. It was built with imported materials and employed foreign artisans who were gifted in their specialties (see 1 Kgs 7:13–14, for example).

Over the years there were probably many changes involving both internal and external refurbishings, and this accounts in part for the confusing information we have in the bible describing the temple. It stood for almost four hundred years in times of changing social, military, and economic environments. During these centuries it is even possible to visualize the temple as rising and falling in the esteem of the population of both Jerusalem and Judah.

One story of a temple change concerns King Ahaz, and it has the ring of historical truth.

> When King Ahaz went to Damascus to meet King Tiglath-pileser of Assyria, he saw the altar that was at Damascus. King Ahaz sent to the priest Uriah a model of the altar and its pattern exact in all its details. (2 Kgs 16:10–11)

Why was Ahaz in Damascus to meet Tiglath-pileser? He was probably there under command from the Assyrian king to learn how to be an Assyrian vassal. We know he was gone from Jerusalem long enough for Uriah to complete the construction of the altar before he returned to Jerusalem. Ahaz ordered the bronze altar that had been placed in its central position in the days of Solomon to be moved to the north side of the temple. He also made other alterations (2 Kgs 16:17–18). Scholars have been influenced by the closing words of the account, which read:

> He [Ahaz] did this because of the king of Assyria. (2 Kgs 16:18)

The above words constitute an editorial comment. It is highly unlikely that the king of Assyria would have had any interest in the changes Ahaz ordered. Notice that in the account there is nothing to indicate that Ahaz was pressured to send the altar model to Uriah. It was his own idea. During the reign of Ahaz, Isaiah of Jerusalem was alive. In Isaiah's oracles there is not a hint of condemnation directed to Ahaz for his temple alterations. Changes in the temple were part of a normal evolutionary process. The historian believed that the kings of Judah had the right to change temple structure and temple practices.

An example of changing temple practice is recorded for us in the introduction of Hezekiah's reign.

> He [Hezekiah] broke in pieces the bronze serpent that Moses had made, for until those days the people of Israel had made offerings to it; it was called Nehushtan. (2 Kgs 18:4)

In spite of the fact that an attempt was made to historicize this cultic object (Nm 21:8–9), its origin is buried in Israel's Canaanite past.

There is a long-standing dispute among scholars concerning the beginning of Hezekiah's reign. Some chronologies state that Hezekiah began his reign in 727 before the destruction of Samaria by the Assyrians, and others state that Hezekiah began his reign in 715.[7] We are not going to review this problem. Sufficient for our purpose is to note that shortly after the destruction of the northern kingdom, significant events took place during the reign of Hezekiah.

NOTES

1. While it is true that there is a third-person account of a visit to Bethel by Amos, where Bethel is called "the king's sanctuary, and…a temple of the kingdom" (Am 7:13), this is not a part of DH, and Amos is not mentioned in DH. References to Bethel in Amos were added to the scroll of Amos a century after Amos died to further discredit the shrine during the reign of Josiah. In this Amos story the priest of Bethel forbids a true prophet of Yahweh to speak.

The status of Bethel had to be affected by the establishment of Samaria as the grand capital city of Israel by Omri, who began his reign in 876 B.C.E.

2. Whether there were twelve or thirteen rulers in Judah during the length of Israel's existence depends on the chronology for Hezekiah's reign. The chronology used in the *NJBC* has 715 for the beginning of Hezekiah's reign. Some other chronologies have Hezekiah beginning his reign in 729 or 727. Information for Hezekiah's reign is contradictory in Kings.

3. There are a few kings for whom the name of the mother is not supplied.

4. While there was a quasi-official role for the king's mother, there was no official role for the king's wife unless she became the mother of the next king. Consult the article in *SBL, Journal of Biblical Literature* 112, no. 3 (Fall

1993), entitled "The Queen Mother and the Cult in Ancient Israel," by Susan Ackerman.

5. Although the Hebrew words *qades* and *qedesa* are commonly interpreted as male and female cult prostitutes, this translation has been questioned. See R. Odin's book, *The Bible Without Theology*, pp. 131–53. Also, consult two articles that appear in *The Anchor Bible Dictionary* under the heading "Prostitution" vol. 5, pp. 505–13. Archaeologist Ephraim Stern, in an article entitled "What Happened to the Cult Figurines?" (*BAR,* July/August, 1989), states that Greek sources have confirmed sacred prostitution at Dor, a Phoenician coastal town not far from Megiddo and Taanach (p. 53).

6. See the article on *tabernacle* in the *Harper's Bible Dictionary* by Joshua R. Porter on p. 1013.

7. For example, the *Harper's Bible Dictionary* states that the reign of Hezekiah began in 727, while the *New Jerome Biblical Commentary* gives the date as 715. See note 2 above.

18

Refugees from Israel in Jerusalem

Shortly before the reign of Hezekiah (or during his reign, if Hezekiah's monarchy started in 727 B.C.E.), groups of refugees from the crumbling northern kingdom of Israel began to appear in the south, especially in the area of Jerusalem. The population of Jerusalem and its suburbs increased substantially during the last quarter of the eighth century.

One of the groups that surfaced in Jerusalem was a circle of zealous Levitical priests and scribes from the Shechem area that was going to change both the character and the practice of religion in Jerusalem and throughout Judah. The theological descendants of this circle would become known to modern scholars as the Deuteronomic circle and, later, the Deuteronomists, but they never called themselves by these names. To understand the revolutionary views of this circle of Levitical priests, we will briefly review information from their past and future. From their past we will review the information they have provided for us concerning the days of Jeroboam, the first king of the northern nation-state of Israel; and from their future (after the reign of Hezekiah), we will highlight the distinctive theological views of the scrolls they and their continuing school produced, scrolls that contained unique and powerful theological concepts.

Review: Rehoboam at Shechem

Following the death of Solomon, Solomon's son went to Shechem to negotiate his acceptance as king of all Israel (1 Kgs 12:1). Why did Rehoboam go to Shechem of all places to become king, since Jerusalem was the capital city and the only logical location for his coronation? This is a reasonable question. A reasonable answer is that the priests of Shechem (a Levitical priesthood) spoke for the oppressed rural masses of Israel. It is our belief that the Shechemites were responsible for uniting the farmers and citizens of Israel in a rebellion against the unfair, abusive policies of Solomon, including heavy taxation to support the monarchy and forced labor (corvée). When Rehoboam refused to negotiate, the Shechemite priesthood supported Jeroboam as an alternative monarch. Shortly after his coronation, however, Jeroboam decided that he was not willing to reign under the domination of the Levite social agenda and moved his capital from Shechem to Penuel.[1]

> ...he [Jeroboam] went out from there [Shechem] and built Penuel.
> (1 Kgs 12:25)

Penuel proved to be only a temporary capital for Israel, and the capital was later moved to Tirzah. Early in Jeroboam's reign he designated Bethel and Dan as the official shrines of the new nation-state, thereby disfranchising the Levitical priesthood of Shechem.

> Jeroboam appointed priests from among the people who were not Levites. (1 Kgs 12:31)...Jeroboam did not turn from his evil ways, but made priests for the high places from among all the people; any who wanted to become priests he consecrated for the high places. (1 Kgs 13:33)

The rejection of the Levitical priesthood of Shechem was the best thing that happened to the future population of Israel and Judah. This break with the monarchy allowed the Shechemites to maintain their theological view of Yahweh as a god of the powerless, and on this foundation they would eventually produce a theology and a collection of scrolls that would change not only the theology of Judah but the entire western world. For a period of 285 years, from the break with Jeroboam to the reign of Josiah (and even further), this school was able to develop a Yahwist theology free from the necessity of bolstering royal propaganda and supporting an elite ruling class. Their theology, which would surface briefly during the reign of Hezekiah and fully during the reign of Josiah, was developed outside of and in reaction to the official state government.

Hezekiah's Reign

One of the first things we notice about the description of Hezekiah's reign is the mention of Moses three times (2 Kgs 18:4, 6, 12). Nothing like this appears in the account of any king after Solomon's death until Hezekiah.[2] The mention of Moses (the Deuteronomic lawgiver), along with a statement concerning Hezekiah's destruction of the high places (18:4), may indicate the influence of the Shechemite Levitical priests in Jerusalem and has led some scholars to the conclusion that the preexilic edition of DH appeared, not during the reign of

Josiah, but during the reign of Hezekiah.[3] These scholars quote the words below to support their position.

> ...there was no one like him [Hezekiah] among all the kings of Judah after him, or among those who were before him. (2 Kgs 18:5)

It is possible that Hezekiah did in fact carry on a Josiah-like reform, and there is a tradition in 2 Chronicles 30 that praises Hezekiah for keeping a nationwide passover to which he invited the citizens of the north (Israel). The historicity of Hezekiah's passover has to be questioned if we believe the account of Josiah's later national passover in Jerusalem.

> No such passover had been kept since the days of the judges who judged Israel. (2 Kgs 23:22)[4]

Hezekiah's reform is described as follows:

> He removed the high places, broke down the pillars, and cut down the sacred poles. (2 Kgs 18:4)

It is in conjunction with Hezekiah's reform that the reader (listener) is informed that Hezekiah destroyed the bronze serpent that Moses had made, Nehushtan. This Moses tradition (Nm 21:1–9) was entirely incompatible with the Shechemite portrayal of Moses as a lawgiver and prophet-statesman. It is entirely possible that the destruction of the cultic object was the result of the influence on Hezekiah of the Levitical refugees from Shechem.

The Siege of Jerusalem by Sennacherib

The description of Hezekiah's reign in the canonical version of DH differs from the description of the reigns of previous kings. Beginning with the invasion of Judah by the Assyrians, three stories of Hezekiah interacting with Isaiah of Jerusalem are presented (2 Kgs 18:13–20:19). These same stories almost word for word appear in the scroll of Isaiah (chapters 36–39). They are:

(1) The Siege of Jerusalem
(2) The Illness of Hezekiah
(3) The Visit of the Babylonian Envoys

The three incidents are not in chronological order. The visit of the Babylonian envoys, which is last, probably took place first, before 710.[5] It is our belief that these three stories did not reach their canonical form until after the death of Josiah and almost a century after the death of Isaiah.

A Yahweh-Only Priesthood

In this book we have maintained that the predominant religion of Israel was polytheistic both at the scattered rural high places and at official state-sanctioned shrines at Bethel, Samaria, and Jerusalem. It is when we review the theology of the Josianic Deuteronomic circle that we first encounter the bold belief that Yahweh is the only god who should be worshiped in Israel/Judah. In their introduction (Deuteronomy) to DH we read:

> I am Yahweh your God, who brought you out of the land of Egypt…you shall have no other gods before me. (Dt 5:6)

> Hear O Israel: Yahweh is our God, Yahweh alone. (Dt 6:4)

That the Deuteronomic circle was a *Yahweh-only* circle there can be no doubt. The question we cannot answer is when these former Shechemites *become* a Yahweh-only party. Did they champion Yahweh as the only god of Israel before they fled the Assyrian invasion of the north, or did they reach their conclusion after settling in Judah, following a passage of time? We cannot say with assurance. The fact that they brought with them the original oracles of Amos and Hosea and later expanded and updated these oracles in their scroll collection indicates that they were strong champions of Yahweh. Were they further influenced by the oracles of Isaiah of Jerusalem and Micah of Moresheth? Did they have a clear theological interpretation of the fall of Israel and the tragic events of 722 when they arrived in Jerusalem, or did their theology develop after decades of reflection and study? These are matters on which we can only speculate.

What the Levites Found When They Came South to Jerusalem

When the disfranchised Levitical priesthood of Shechem arrived in Jerusalem they encountered firsthand aspects of Jerusalem theology that they may have been familiar with from a distance. These would have included the following:

(1) The official state religion was set forth in the capital city of Jerusalem, a city closely tied to the house of David.
(2) Jerusalem was dominated by a large Syrian-type temple that was close to the royal palace.
(3) The temple was in the control of a strong professional priesthood, believed to be descended from Zadok, which promoted a royal Davidic theology.
(4) Yahweh, introduced to Jerusalem by David, the founder of the dynasty, was a primary god of the temple and had absorbed the majestic qualities of El, a high god of Canaanite tradition.

(5) There was a well-established belief that David's Yahweh had chosen the temple on Mount Zion as his dwelling.

(6) Other gods were honored in the temple, including Baal and Asherah.

(7) Just as in Israel, in the rural areas of Judah there were multiple high places staffed by independent priesthoods with a variety of religious practices. These locations may have included Mizpah, Gibeon, Bethshemesh, Hebron, Lachish, Arad, and Beersheba.

What the Levites Brought with Them from Shechem

DH informs us of the attempted reforms of Hezekiah, but we don't know how historical this account is. We have stated above that some scholars have hinted at an early copy of a proto-DH, starting with David and ending with Hezekiah, but we are not convinced of this speculation. If the Hezekiah reform account is true and produced by Levitical action, then these Levites of Shechem brought with them a ready-made reformation spirit that could have produced the aborted reform of Hezekiah but that could hardly have been capable of success in changing the entrenched beliefs of Jerusalem. They were newly arrived outsiders without a real feeling for the environment in which they found themselves. And they had not been successful in their own culture at taking charge and affecting religious belief and practice outside their own territory.

At this point in our review (the reign of Hezekiah), we are going to take a conservative view of the theology of this school. From *the later output* of this influential group, we can identify firm, outstanding viewpoints, but our feeling is that these mature viewpoints could easily have developed in Jerusalem after the reign of Hezekiah, during the seventh century, culminating in the reign of Josiah.

They may have brought the following theological concepts with them from Shechem:

(1) Yahweh was viewed as a unique warrior god who had fought for Israel in the past and was a champion of the powerless.

(2) Yahweh was conceived of as a god of law.

(3) This group was in the early stages of recognizing the great importance of writings in the future of Israelite religion.

(4) When the members of this circle arrived in Jerusalem, they had a modest view of the place of animal and agricultural sacrifices and were shocked by the great amount of sacrificial activity at the Jerusalem temple.

(5) Their view of Moses was very human. He was a statesman and a lawgiver. The chest he had made for the torah was a simple wooden chest, not an ornate ark with winged cherubim and covered with gold, as described in Exodus 25:10–22.

(6) While they may not have been a Yahweh-only circle, they certainly were moving in that direction.

In their new home they became familiar with the statements of several prominent teachers, Isaiah of Jerusalem and Micah of Moresheth, oracles of which they have preserved for us. In our next chapter we will try to imagine how the views of the Shechemites were influenced by Isaiah and Micah as time passed.

NOTES

1. I have written a book explaining why I believe that the Levitical priesthood of Shechem provided the theological ancestry for the Deuteronomic circle of the late seventh century that produced both the book of Deuteronomy and the Deuteronomic history (DH), *Obsession with Justice: The Story of the Deuteronomists* (Mahwah, N.J.: Paulist Press, 1994).

2. In the description of the reign of Amaziah, a law attributed to Moses is mentioned (2 Kgs 14:6).

3. See the conclusions of Weippert and Provan as summarized by Steven McKenzie in his book *The Trouble with Kings* (1991), pp. 117–22.

4. It is my view that there may have been an early effort by the Levitical priestly circle to influence Hezekiah to conduct a reform of religious practices in Judah and that a document we could call proto-DH was used to support Hezekiah. This short scroll would have started with David and ended with Hezekiah. The end of the eighth century would have been too early for the Shechemite Levitical circle to put together anything as massive as DH, beginning with Joshua (and later ending with Josiah).

5. For a discussion of these three incidents and the time of their composition, see my book *Isaiah of Jerusalem* (Paulist Press, 1992).

19

Isaiah and Micah

There must have been orators and public proclaimers in Judah before the latter part of the eighth century whose oracles were worth preserving on scrolls. The fact that the first two turned out to be Isaiah and Micah supports our time estimate that the Shechemites arrived in Jerusalem during the last days of the eighth century and that they placed a great value on writings. The presence of Deuteronomic vocabulary and Deuteronomic theology in the canonical scrolls of Isaiah and Micah (as well as Amos and Hosea) further supports this.

Several aspects of the poetic oracles of Isaiah would have appealed to the Shechemite Levites: (a) Isaiah's vision of Yahweh in the Temple supported the Yahweh-only direction in which the Levites were heading; and (b) Isaiah, like Hosea, was a severe critic of foreign alliances in place of complete trust in Yahweh as Israel's (Judah's) ancient god of war.

Twelve years or more before the tragic events of 722 (the fall of Israel), the Levitical priests of Shechem first heard of Isaiah of Jerusalem. In 737 Rezin, king of Syria, took a leadership role in the formation of an anti-Assyrian coalition. Pekah, king of Israel (737–732), who had seized the throne by assassination, willingly joined this anti-Assyrian coalition, and the plan was to enlist the cooperation of King Ahaz of Judah. Ahaz refused to join the coalition. Isaiah supported Ahaz in this position. Rezin and Pekah devised a plan to march on Jerusalem and replace Ahaz as king with someone identified as the son of Tabeel (Is 7:6). Both the book of Isaiah and DH record for us that Isaiah, a poet of influence in Jerusalem, supported Ahaz in his decision not to join the coalition, in spite of the threat from Pekah and Rezin.

Isaiah's encouragement of Ahaz was based on his belief that Yahweh would not allow Syria and Israel to capture Jerusalem or to replace Ahaz. Ahaz was challenged to trust Yahweh as the deliverer of Jerusalem and the preserver of the house of David. The anti-Assyrian alliance was destroyed when the Assyrian army under the leadership of Tiglath-pileser marched west and dealt a punishing blow to Syria and Israel. Both Rezin and Pekah were killed. Pekah, king of Israel, was killed by the man who would become the final king of Israel, Hoshea (732–722). Hoshea started his reign as a vassal of Assyria.

If the above account is accurate as reported in Isaiah and DH, it is likely that the Levitical priests of Shechem, also champions of Yahweh, would have been stirred by Isaiah's leadership. When they fled to Jerusalem a few years later, they would have already had a great curiosity about this champion of Yahweh.

Although the Shechemites would have been stirred by Isaiah's emphasis on Yahweh and his warrior-god character, their northern rural setting would not prepare them for other temple-centered concepts held by Isaiah.[1] It is possible that their theological views, developed over a long period of time as a disfranchised cult, meant that they brought to Jerusalem antimonarchical sentiments that would be subject to reexamination.

In chapter 18 we provided two lists contrasting what the Shechemites encountered when they arrived in Jerusalem and what they brought with them. Under no circumstances would these northern Levitical priests have been comfortable with the concept that Yahweh had desired a dwelling place in the temple and actually lived in the Holy of Holies.[2] In their later writings they would continue to vehemently oppose this theology. They would add these words to Solomon's dedicatory prayer for the temple:

> But will God indeed dwell on the earth? Even heaven and the highest heaven cannot contain you, much less this house that I have built. (1 Kgs 8:27)

We know from their later writings that they ultimately compromised with the Jerusalem theology in the production of their *name theology*. The God of Israel would not dwell in the temple. Only his name would dwell there. Solomon is then quoted as saying,

> ...that your eyes [LORD] may be open day and night toward this house, the place of which you said, My name shall dwell there. (1 Kgs 8:29)

And Deuteronomy repeatedly speaks of

> ...the place that the LORD God will choose as a dwelling for his name. (Dt 12:11).

The above illustration (concerning the name theology) gives us insight into how the Israelite refugees resisted a theological concept that Isaiah would have been comfortable with. But this influential circle would make compromises with Jerusalem theology as time passed. As a matter of fact, that body of theological belief that would make such an impact on Judahite theology beginning in the late-seventh-century reign of Josiah—known much later as the Deuteronomic viewpoint—can best be understood as the result (but not the *end result*) of the interaction between the Shechemites and the official theology of Jerusalem. An example of a compromise would be related to their antimonarchic sentiments. They would soften their anti-monarchic feelings when they later realized that the preservation of the house of David would best serve the people of Judah and the Yahweh-only doctrine on which they would first build their quest for centralization and standardization.

Identifying Isaiah's Oracles

We would like to know in what ways the oracles of Isaiah influenced the Levitical circle that first arrived in Jerusalem close to the tragic events of 722, but there is a problem. This is the group that preserved for us the oracles of Isaiah (and Amos and Hosea). Most modern scholars agree that the oracles of the eighth-century spokespersons (later called prophets, see chapter 23) have been heavily redacted (edited) by this school. And there is wide disagreement in identifying the original oracles of Isaiah apart from later Deuteronomistic additions, interpretations, and revisions.

However, there are characteristics of Isaiah of Jerusalem's oracles that distinguish them from the other eighth-century prophets. These include the following:

(1) Isaiah's oracles have as their center the mystical experience of his vision of Yahweh in the temple (Is 6). This first-person account continues in chapter 8 through verse 18.

> See, I and the children whom the LORD has given me are signs and portents in Israel from the LORD of hosts, who dwells on Mount Zion.

(2) The beauty and power of Isaiah's poetry are unsurpassed. Read, for example, the vivid description of the invading Assyrian army in 5:24–30. Or read the stirring coronation speech of 9:2–7 beginning with the words,

> The people who walked in darkness have seen a great light.

Or the oracle called "the Peaceful Kingdom" in 11:1–9. Isaiah was Israel's greatest poet.

(3) Isaiah had a particular contempt for human pride and arrogance, be it Judahite, Israelite, Assyrian, or Egyptian (Is 2:12–17, 10:7–19, 13:11, 14:12–17, 28:1–4).

(4) For protection and survival Isaiah was adamant that Judah should trust in Yahweh and avoid alliances with military powers such as Egypt (Is 30:1–5). As we have said, this was the view of Hosea also.

(5) Like Amos, Isaiah would see the punishment of Israel delivered by the Assyrian army as the result of Yahweh's wrath. Assyria would be the rod in Yahweh's hand. Yahweh is quoted as saying,

> Ah, Assyria, the rod of my anger—
> the club in their hands is my fury!
> Against a godless nation I send him,
> and against the people of my wrath I command him,
> to take spoil and seize plunder,
> and to tread them down like the mire of the
> streets. (Is 10:5–6)

This understanding of Yahweh's power, based on his ancient warrior-god character, would remove the boundaries of his might and result in his promotion from a local god to an international power.[3]

We should not assume that because Isaiah championed Yahweh as a result of his vision, that non-Yahwistic practices disappeared in Judah. The authentic oracles of Isaiah appear in the first thirty-three chapters of the book of Isaiah, and not once is there a word of condemnation of the high places. The same practices of high places (later called abominable) that we listed in chapter 13 continued throughout Judah.[4] In reviewing the sins of Israel (the northern kingdom), an editor has added these words:

> Judah also did not keep the commandments of the LORD their God
> but walked in the customs that Israel had introduced. (2 Kgs
> 17:19)

Of course, Israel had not *introduced* these customs to Judah. They were indigenous to Judah, just as they had been indigenous to Israel, part of Judah's Canaanite heritage.

Micah of Moresheth

The oracles of Micah would have attracted the attention of the Shechemites because of the similarity of their viewpoint to the oracles of Amos. Like Amos, Micah was a voice of severe criticism addressing the decision makers of the capital city because of their economic policies, which resulted in severe poverty and hardship for the rural farmers of Judah.

Micah is the only eighth-century spokesperson who has the distinction of being quoted by the seventh-century champion of Yahweh, Jeremiah:

Micah of Moresheth, who prophesied during the days of King
Hezekiah of Judah, said to all the people of Judah: "Thus says the
LORD of hosts: Zion shall be plowed as a field; Jerusalem shall
become a heap of ruins, and the mountain of the house a wooded
height." (Jer 26:18)

Although Jeremiah says that Micah spoke to *all the people of Judah,* a reading
of the original oracle of Micah shows that it was directed to the elite decision
makers in positions of power, supporting our statement that those who were
recognized as eighth-century prophets addressed, not the people, but the polit-
ically powerful of the capital cities:

> Hear this you rulers of the house of Jacob
>   and chiefs of the house of Israel,
> who abhor justice and pervert all equity
>   who build Zion with blood and Jerusalem with
> wrong. (Mi 3:9–10)

Like Amos, Micah was a social critic who directed his oracles against
the urban decision makers who profited by exploitation of the powerless. Like
Amos, Micah is livid and specific when he speaks to issues of economic injustice he experiences:

> …you rise against my people as an enemy;
> you strip the robe from the peaceful
> …the women of my people you drive out of their pleasant houses;
> and from their young children you take away my glory forever.
> (Mi 2:8–9)[5]

The Shechemites and Writings

According to our time schedule, the Levitical priests and scribes from
Shechem arrived in Jerusalem in time to encounter both Isaiah and Micah.
They also left Israel late enough to have heard Amos and Hosea. It was this
circle, beginning to realize the important place that written scrolls would play
in the future of their theological program, that preserved for us the oracles of
these teachers. There may have been other prominent spokespersons in the
north and the south whose words died with them, but the oracles of these four
(Amos, Hosea, Isaiah, and Micah) found a resonance in the hearts of the
Shechemites. Both Amos and Micah spoke for the powerless, the rural poor
whose lives were being destroyed for the luxury and comfort of an urban elite.
Both Hosea and Isaiah criticized the decision makers of the two capital cities,
the monarch and his advisors, when alliances with foreign military powers

were pursued and Yahweh was disregarded and forgotten as the warrior god of ancient Israel.

Also, as we have suggested above, the timing was right for this circle to have influenced Hezekiah in the destruction of the bronze serpent (Nehushtan) attributed to the ownership of Moses, a Moses whose identity clashed with the Shechemite identity of Moses. Their Moses was a statesperson and lawgiver, not a worker of magic.[6] If our guess is right, the destruction of Nehushtan would have been the first act of reformation in Judah of this Levitical priesthood.

A Scroll of Laws

One of the things the Shechemites brought with them to Judah was a view that Yahweh was a god concerned with law. It is reasonable to assume that with their growing appreciation of written scrolls they would have had a scroll of just laws. If there is any truth to the tradition of Hezekiah's short-lived reform, the question is, Was there a body of law underlying the reform, such as the Book of the Law *(sepher hattorah),* which would later undergird the reforms of Josiah? If so, it may have been the Book of the Covenant[7] later found in Exodus 20:22–23:33. R. E. Clements, in his commentary on Exodus, suggests that the Book of the Covenant was a standard of law for a particular region. He says specifically, "the region settled by Ephraim, with its center at Shechem, would be most likely."[8]

In keeping with a common practice, we will refer to the Book of the Covenant as BC. BC contained ancient agricultural laws, but it also contained other laws added much later. Early laws would include those that forbade steps to an altar, assuming that lay persons without proper undergarments would be making sacrifices rather than priests who would be properly dressed. BC also contained several agricultural laws concerning oxen. The law against cursing a chief *(nasi)* would later be expanded to cover cursing the king (1 Kgs 21:10). Only males are required to attend the three-times-a-year pilgrimage festivals in BC. Someone reading BC will picture a primitive agricultural setting.[9]

But there are many evidences of updating in BC. Debt slavery was a problem of the eighth century, as was the protection of aliens in Judah.[10] Judicial officials are forbidden to receive a bribe, and professional money lenders are restricted in their practices with the poor. If a master has a female slave and does not desire her as a wife, he may designate her for his son. In this case he must treat her as a daughter. This protects the female slave and reminds us of the eighth-century complaint of Amos:

> ...father and son go in to the same girl so that my name is profaned. (Am 2:7)

Both civil and cultic laws have been updated in BC. For this reason we cannot point to laws demanding the exclusive worship of Yahweh in BC as pre-monarchical or even early monarchical.

Sixty years after the death of Hezekiah, another son of the house of David, Josiah, would attempt a complete reform of religious practices in Judah accompanied by an attempt to reunite the northern territory, formerly known as Israel. A much-improved torah, a collection of laws (at least parts of Dt 12–26), would undergird this later reform. The Deuteronomic torah would incorporate about 50 percent of BC, but the clarity and impact of its opening section would distinguish it as a demanding, new approach to theological understanding in Judah.

NOTES

1. Of course, the center of Isaiah's experience was built around his vision of Yahweh in the temple (Is 6).

2. At the time of the dedication of the temple, Solomon is quoted as saying, "The LORD has said that he would dwell in thick darkness. I have built you an exalted house, a place for you to dwell in."

3. Isaiah's view of Assyria as a rod in Yahweh's hand and then an arrogant power worthy of Yahweh's wrath produced a logical explanation for the ambivalent feelings that Judahites would have had toward Assyria.

4. 2 Kings 17:7–18.

5. A century later, the Josianic editor of Micah added the words below. He perceived Yahweh as a God who was obsessed with obedience to the law (the torah) and social order:

He has told you, O mortal what is good;
and what does the LORD require of you
but to do justice, and to love kindness,
and to walk humbly with your God? (Mi 6:8)

6. Notice that the bronze serpent incident is not included in the DH section found in the book of Isaiah, which, we stated, was written seven decades after Hezekiah's death.

7. The name *Book of the Covenant* is unfortunate. The collection is called the Book of the Covenant because of a sentence in Exodus 24:7 that states that Moses "took the book of the covenant, and read it in the hearing of the people." I am suggesting that the scroll of laws brought to Jerusalem by the Levitical priests of Shechem was not called the Book of the Covenant until much later than the late eighth century, let alone as early as the lifetime of Moses.

8. Ronald E. Clements, *The Cambridge Bible Commentary: Exodus* (Cambridge: Cambridge University Press, 1972), p. 128.

9. Brevard Childs, *Exodus*, pp. 456–57. Childs also points out that BC was not part of the Sinai tradition and contains Deuteronomic glosses (p. 454).

10. These aliens may very well have been Israelites fleeing to Judah after the fall of Israel.

20

Sixty Years of Silence

For a period of sixty years, beginning with the final days of Hezekiah's life and continuing through the long reign of Manasseh, the historian decided to tell us almost nothing. It is a period of silence. A much later historian, the chronicler, would report that interesting things happened during these first six decades of the seventh century. King Manasseh, he tells us, was carried in manacles to Babylon by the king of Assyria.[1] The chronicler further reports that, while in captivity, Manasseh repented and found favor with Yahweh his god (2 Chr 33:10–13). A lot of things can happen during a fifty-five-year reign.

The DH period of silence ends abruptly with several acts of unexpected violence shortly after the acquisition of the throne by Manasseh's son Amon (642).

> The servants of Amon conspired against him and killed the king in his house. But the people of the land killed all those who had conspired against King Amon....(2 Kgs 21:23–24)

The people of the land who executed the conspirators were not the rural peasants of Judah, but a group of landowners referred to in *NJBC* as the Judean gentry. But this informs us that there were parties with vested interests in Jerusalem during the second half of the seventh century, interests intense enough to result in an assassination and later execution.

For the DH historian, Manasseh was more valuable as a straw man. He is completely an example of an ungodly Judean leader with no redeeming features, a complete contrast to Hezekiah, his father, and Josiah, his grandson. The report of Manasseh's reign (2 Kgs 21) states that he rebuilt the high places that his father Hezekiah had destroyed. This is very unlikely. Why would a son of the house of David living in Jerusalem want to rebuild the scattered shrines of Judah?[2] The account goes on to say that he worshiped all the host of heaven and served them. The worship of the sun, moon, and stars as gods was encouraged by Assyrian influence, and it was probably not considered an evil practice until the reign of Josiah. Manasseh is accused of some of the superstitious practices common among the rural population of Judah.

> ...he practiced soothsaying and augury, and dealt with mediums
> and with wizards. (2 Kgs 21:6)

A reference to a carved image of Asherah that Manasseh had ordered for the Jerusalem temple reminds us that the goddess, thought by some scholars to be known as a consort of Yahweh,[3] was just as much at home in the Jerusalem royal temple as she was in the scattered high places of Judah.[4]

To complete the picture, Manasseh is reported to have made his son pass through fire.[5]

So for the fifty-five- (or forty-five-) year reign of Manasseh, we have only nine verses in DH, most condemning religious practices of Judah. Other condemnatory material was added later. The reason we would like to have more information about this period is that it was during this time that the Shechemite priesthood was transformed into the Deuteronomic circle. Since we have so little information, we have to speculate, whether we like it or not. Some scholars begin their speculation by suggesting that the reformation attempt of Hezekiah fits the timetable for the arrival in Jerusalem of the Shechemite priests and scribes. Some have suggested that an early version of DH (proto-DH) may have supported Hezekiah's reform and that this early version of DH may have started with David and ended with Hezekiah.[6] Supporting this theory, that an early form of DH started with David, is the fact that each king of Judah is compared with David and declared good or evil in accordance with his compliance with or departure from David's obedience to Yahweh. In the last chapter we mentioned that the Shechemites would have been interested in Isaiah's support for the temple and the house of David. This comes out in a Deuteronomic introduction to the oracles of Isaiah (Is 1), where the early reign of David in Jerusalem is viewed as a golden age.[7]

> How the faithful city has become a whore!
> She *that was full of justice,*
>   righteousness lodged in her—
> ...I will restore your judges as at the first,
>   and your counselors as at the beginning.
> Afterward you shall be called the city of
>   righteousness, the faithful city. (Is 1:21, 26)

The weakness of the view that the Shechemites sparked the reformation of Hezekiah is simply this: The Shechemites were small in number and would not have had time to build a position of strength for themselves where they would have been able to influence the type of reform ascribed to Hezekiah. Knowing how history was written in those days makes it possible that the reform activity of Hezekiah was a later idealization of Hezekiah's reign.

The Priests of Jerusalem

The priests of the Jerusalem temple are sometimes referred to as Zadokites, or the sons of Zadok. A tradition of David tells us that David appointed Abiathar and Zadok to be priests of the Jerusalem shrine (2 Sm 8:17). Later we are informed that Solomon dismissed Abiathar and banished him from Jerusalem[8] because he supported Adonijah as David's successor. Zadok supported Solomon.

The background of Zadok is vague. Some scholars think that Zadok was a priest of Hebron, David's first capital.[9] Other scholars believe that Zadok was a Jebusite priest of Jerusalem, predating David's capture of the city.[10] In many scholarly discussions the student may get the idea that there were only two types of priesthoods in ancient Israel, Levite and Zadokite, or three types, Levite, Zadokite, and Aaronite.[11] Our previous assumptions in this book rule out this oversimplification. There were not two or three priesthoods. There were innumerable priesthoods through the centuries, of great diversity, perhaps as many priesthoods as there were rural high places.[12]

The idealization of unity projected into Israel's ancient past, first by the historian author of DH and later by the chronicler and the P (priestly) source, has not only confused the student but has affected the writings of innumerable scholars. In early Israel there were no committees on orthodoxy and no central authority to determine what constituted an authentic priesthood. It is more logical to believe that some priesthoods emerged gradually in local areas as Israel grew and that other priesthoods were able to trace their origin to the Canaanite past. Some scholars talk about the theology of the Levites. By this they mean the theology of the Shechemite Levites. Levites from other locations may have developed entirely different theologies. The meaning of the term *Levite* itself is buried in Israel's antiquity, and the references to ancient Levites are contradictory.[13] It is our guess that in many locations the term Levite was a generic term for priest. In the book of Deuteronomy, all priests are assumed to be Levites.[14]

In the last years of the monarchy, when the first edition of the Deuteronomic history appeared, the historian's attention was entirely on Jerusalem. Jerusalem was the place that Yahweh had chosen for his name to dwell. Because the historian considered himself a priest or scribe of a Levitical priesthood and because the priesthood of Jerusalem consisted of the sons of Zadok, it became inevitable that these two priesthoods would be identified and emphasized in subsequent writings to the exclusion of other priesthoods, many of which would already have perished with the demise of the northern kingdom.

How Were the Priests of Shechem Received in Jerusalem?

The arrival of the Shechemite Levites in Jerusalem would have caused no immediate problems. The Zadokite priests of Jerusalem were the most professional of priests. They surely exceeded in size the priesthoods of the rural high places of Judah and were better educated. Being located in Jerusalem would have insured this. Because of their strongly entrenched position in Jerusalem, it is safe to assume that the arrival in Jerusalem of the Shechemite Levitical priesthood would have caused no feelings of apprehension. On the contrary, it is my belief that the Shechemites would have been greeted with curiosity and courtesy. Their party was rural and small in number, perhaps ten or twelve priests accompanied by wives and children. They brought scrolls with them that would have been of interest to some of the Zadokites. Their curiosity about Isaiah, the poet laureate of Judah, may have been announced, and their reputation as Israelite opponents of the shrine at Bethel may have been common knowledge in Jerusalem. This would have put them in a favorable light. Bethel was a competing shrine with Jerusalem. And at least some of the royal priests would have been curious about the views of these Levites, including their perception of Yahweh as a god preoccupied with obedience to a revealed body of law. The scroll of law that the Shechemites brought with them to Jerusalem was some form of the Book of the Covenant that later would make its appearance in the scroll of Exodus (20:22–23:33). Martin Noth wrote as follows:

> ...at some time which can no longer be discovered with any accuracy the "Book of the Covenant" has been inserted into the Sinai section [of Exodus].[15]

From Shechemite Levites to Deuteronomic Circle

During the reign of Manasseh, the Levites of Shechem, now living in Jerusalem, began to internalize the tremendous impact that the destruction of Israel (and Shechem) had had on their lives and their theology. To their own small collection of writings, scrolls of Amos and Hosea and a scroll of law (BC), they added the oracles of two Judean teachers, Isaiah and Micah. There were profound theological questions raised by the destruction of Israel, and for answers they studied their scrolls. If Hosea was right that reliance for military protection on foreign nations (Egypt and Assyria) was nothing more than trusting in horses and chariots and constituted an unwise, cruel, and undeserved rejection of Yahweh, they could explain (to their own satisfaction) the destruction of Bethel and Samaria. But the total destruction of the entire nation, including Shechem, and the permanent carrying away into humiliating foreign captivity of many of Israel's good people had left them stunned.

Perhaps in the teachings of Isaiah they would find new answers. In the closing years of the eighth century, not long after the demise of Israel, the Assyrian army, under the leadership of Sennacherib, devastated Judah, capturing and inflicting severe damage to more than forty Judean towns, fortresses, and villages.[16] Sennacherib's army moved to the very outskirts of Jerusalem, coming close to repeating the total destruction of Israel in Judah. But the destruction of Judah did not take place. The armies of the Assyrians unexpectedly withdrew, and Sennacherib returned to Nineveh. Sennacherib never returned to the Syria-Palestine area. He was murdered by one of his sons, and the throne was taken by the crown prince, Esarhaddon, in 680.

The withdrawal of Sennacherib and the Assyrian army made a great impact on the Shechemite priests and scribes now living in Jerusalem. The survival of the royal city was a confirmation of Isaiah's teachings concerning the inviolability of Jerusalem.

> Like birds hovering overhead,
> So Yahweh of hosts will protect Jerusalem;
> he will protect it and deliver it,
> he will spare it and rescue it. (Is 31:5)

The inevitable review, growth, and metamorphosis of their Levite theology was influenced by the following:

(a) The failure of the Syro-Ephraimitic coalition to prevail against Jerusalem during the reign of Ahaz.
(b) The oracles of Isaiah of Jerusalem.
(c) The total destruction of Israel by Shalmaneser V and Sargon II.
(d) The failure of Sennacherib to destroy Jerusalem after the capture and destruction of forty-six cities and towns of Judah.
(e) Their encounter with Zion theology and Davidic royal theology.

During the long reign of Manasseh, there would be inevitable changes of personnel in the school of the displaced refugees from Shechem as several generations would come and go. Within the circle that would continue their heritage, a conviction arose that the future of Israel was in their hands and that it was in the best interest of the people of Yahweh to be controlled by a new torah and a new nationalistic theology.

NOTES

1. Assyrian annals seem to support this forced visit to Babylon of Manasseh. See Esarhaddon's prism in *ANET* 294, and see 291, where Manasseh is listed with seacoast kings who were given commands by Esarhaddon.

2. Is it possible that Manasseh would have offered assistance for the rebuilding of high places throughout Judah that may have been damaged by the invasion of Sennacherib in 701? Assistance from the monarch would hardly have been necessary for the restoration of most rural high places. The rural residents and their priests would have been able to rebuild except in those instances where a sizable temple was involved, such as Lachish or, possibly, Beersheba. There is no evidence that Beersheba was rebuilt, however.

3. For a discussion of the relationship between Asherah and Yahweh, see Mark Smith, *The Early History of God*, chapter 3, pp. 80–114; and further, Saul Olyan's book *Âsherah and the Cult of Yahweh in Israel*.

4. Read 2 Kings 23:4–7.
…bring out of the temple of the LORD all the vessels made for Baal, for Asherah, and all the host of heaven….He brought out the image of Asherah from the House of the Lord….He broke down the houses…where the women did weavings for Asherah.

5. The Josianic edition of DH probably ended with verse 9. Later, after the death of Josiah or during the exile, Manasseh was further condemned.
King Manasseh of Judah…has done things more wicked than all that the Amorites did, who were before him, and had caused Judah also to sin with his idols. (2 Kgs 21:11)
Still later Manasseh was accused of shedding much innocent blood in Jerusalem (v. 16).

6. For a discussion of the views of Helga Weippert and Iain Provan—that there was a Hezekian edition of DH, based largely on an examination of the regnal formulas—see McKenzie's book *The Trouble with Kings*, pp. 117–20. This edition is sometimes called DtrH. Another book on this subject is *The Reform of King Josiah* by Erik Eynikel (Leiden: Brill, 1995). Eynikel suggests that DtrH started with Solomon and ended with Hezekiah.

7. There is no doubt that the historian idealized the reign of David. It is in Solomon's reign that all the non-Yahwistic practices are introduced, according to the historian.

8. Abiathar was banished to Anathoth. Later Jeremiah would be known as a son of a priest of Anathoth.

9. See John W. Miller, *The Origins of the Bible*, pp. 53–56.

10. See *New Jerome Biblical Commentary*, pp. 1256–57, for comments on Zadok's Jebusite origins.

11. In exilic and postexilic literature of the Hebrew bible, it is clear that several authors (the chronicler, for example) want the reader or listener to understand without doubt that the sons of Aaron constitute the major priesthood

of the second temple and the Levites are only assistants. In postexilic Tetrateuchal literature (Exodus, Leviticus, Numbers) the reader is told again and again that the main priests of the Tabernacle were the sons of Aaron. See the article "Aaron" by John R. Spencer in the *Anchor Bible Dictionary*, pp. I.1–I.5.

12. This is an exaggeration, of course. It is possible that some rural priesthoods may have officiated at more than one high place.

13. See the story in Exodus 32:21–29. Also, compare Genesis 49:5, where Levi is yoked with Simeon by Jacob's remarks concerning his sons, with Deuteronomy 33:8–11, Moses' blessing for the tribe of Levi.

14. Later, in our discussion of the exilic and postexilic age, we will discuss the phrase *priests and Levites*. The heirs to the royal priests of Jerusalem found it to their advantage, and perhaps they believed for the benefit of restored Judah, to distinguish themselves from other Levites.

15. Martin Noth, *Exodus* (Philadelphia: Westminster, 1962), p. 173.

16. See *ANEP*, pp. 199–201, "The Prism of Sennacherib." Or *ANET*, pp. 287–88.

21

Is the Description of Josiah's Reform Historical?

The account of Josiah's reign as we have it is so well crafted and so exciting that we sometimes overlook the fact that it is made up of many pieces. These include:

1. The temple repair program
2. The discovery of the Book of the Law, the Torah
3. The consultation with Huldah and her prophecy
4. The reading of the Book of the Law to the people
5. A public ceremony of covenant renewal led by Josiah
6. The cleansing of the temple of non-Yahwistic practices
7. The defiling and destruction of the Judean high places from Geba to Beersheba
8. The destruction and defiling of Bethel, a sanctuary singled out for special contempt
9. The dismantling of other high places in the towns of Samaria
10. The holding of a national passover in Jerusalem
11. An attempt to reform local practices that were not carried out at high places, such as the consulting of mediums and the use of household idols
12. The sudden and tragic death of Josiah in battle at Megiddo

It is our belief that the first significant edition of DH started with Joshua and ended with Josiah. Of course, Josiah's untimely death was not part of the plan. For this reason we look for the probable ending of the Josianic edition of DH. It may have consisted of these words.[1]

Before him there was no king like him, who turned to the LORD with all his heart, with all his soul, and with all his might, according to the law of Moses. (2 Kings 23:25)

When we become aware of the many pieces that make up the description of the reign of Josiah, we also become aware that almost any item on the list

---

EXILIC AND POSTEXILIC DATES OF IMPORTANCE

CHART 14

609	Josiah killed at Megiddo. Jerusalem became a vassal of Egypt.
609	Nebuchadnezzer became king of Babylon.
597	Neo-Babylonian (Chaldean) army captured Jerusalem. Many leaders were relocated in captivity.
594/3	Envoys of nations surrounding Judah met in Jerusalem to conspire against Babylonian rule.
587/6	Babylonians destroyed the walls of Jerusalem and razed the temple. More Judeans were taken into captivity.
582	745 more Judeans were relocated to Babylon.
581	Gedaliah, governing at Mizpah, was assassinated, resulting in a flight to Egypt by Judeans who took Jeremiah with them.
561	Jehoiachin, former king of Judah, was released from prison in Babylon and given a position at the king's table.
540	Second Isaiah predicted the release of Judahites from capitvity as a result of Cyrus's victories.
539	Cyrus issued a decree allowing captives to return to their lands.
520–515	The second temple was built in Jerusalem.
445	Nehemiah was appointed governor of Judah.
397	Ezra arrived in Jerusalem with scrolls containing the torah of the Zadokite (Aaronid) priests.

above could have been added after the fact to influence understanding of the attempted reformation. There are enough problems, when a critical approach is applied, to keep graduate students busy into the next century. In this brief book we are not going to devote ourselves to a discussion of these problems, but we will point out a few examples.

1. Chronicles informs us that Josiah started his reforms before the discovery of the Book of the Law, while DH states that the Book of the Law initiated the reformation.
2. The words of Huldah the prophetess—that Josiah would be gathered to his grave in peace—do not seem to be correct. Also, her remarks about the ultimate destruction of Jerusalem would not have encouraged Josiah to put forth his reform effort. Her statement gives the impression that it was crafted after the destruction of Jerusalem.
3. The statement that Josiah led the people in a renewal of the covenant would fit better in a later period after covenant theology was developed as an explanation for the fall of Judah.
4. The book found in the temple is called the *Book of the Law* (2 Kgs 22:11) but later is called the *Book of the Covenant* (2 Kgs 23:2).
5. Would Josiah have had the resources to defile the high places in the towns of Samaria? The northern kingdom was no longer Israelite territory, but a province of Assyria for a century.
6. The reformation as described is so extensive—touching temple practices, reaching to every high place and its priests, and even reforming popular cultic practices that served the people's need to ward off evil spirits, maintain fertility, communicate with the dead, and determine the will of the gods—that whether Josiah had lived or not, complete success would have been too much to expect. It is one thing to determine the best policy for religious belief and practice and quite another to implement this policy.

The above examples serve to illustrate some of the complexities of the account. But there is one controversy we will visit in greater detail. In a recent book entitled *A New Chronology for the Kings of Israel and Judah,*[2] John H. Hayes and Paul K. Hooker state, contrary to the conclusions of most biblical scholars of the last century, that the Book of the Law that was discovered in the temple and that inspired the reformation of Josiah was not a portion of the book of Deuteronomy (proto-Deuteronomy or ur-Deuteronomy) but was a scroll of priestly law (P), and they suggest that the following priestly material may have been included: Exodus 12:1–20, Leviticus 23:4–8, 21–23, and 26. Leviticus 26 states that Yahweh made a covenant with Jacob, Isaac, and Abraham and further cites

...the covenant with their ancestors whom I brought out of the
land of Egypt in the sight of the nations, to be their God: I am the
LORD. (Lv 26:45)

The Torah of the Aaronids

The term *torah* is used in various ways.[3] We are using the term to mean a collection of laws. The royal priests of Jerusalem had a torah, but during Josiah's
reign it was not of the same nature as the torah of the Deuteronomic circle,
which was an early edition of Deuteronomy, chapters 12–26.

The torah of the royal priests was basically a manual for the temple
priesthood. This partial description gives its characteristics.

> This is the ritual of the burnt offering, the grain offering, the sin
> offering, the guilt offering, the offering of ordination, and the sac-
> rifice of well-being. (Lv 7:37)

The torah of the Aaronids was concerned with holiness, something intimately
bound up with moral and physical cleanliness. Holiness could be dangerous
even though it was the opposite of uncleanness.[4] In the Aaronid torah only the
temple priests understood the complications of becoming clean and safe, and
the procedure was intricately involved with priestly rituals involving sacrifices and temple procedures. The Aaronid torah also placed a great emphasis
on diet, which separated Israel for Yahweh and warned against accepting the
ways of non-Israelites.

> ...you shall not bring abomination on yourselves by animal or by
> bird or by anything with which the ground teems, which I have set
> apart for you to hold unclean. You shall be holy to me; for I the
> LORD am holy, and I have separated you from the other peoples to
> be mine. (Lv 20:25–26)

According to the Aaronids, during the wilderness experience Yahweh charged
Aaron to distinguish between the holy and the common (Lv 10:10).

The torah of the Levites (Dt 12–26) was a much more down-to-earth,
practical code, and the royal priests, influenced by the Deuteronomic torah,
later transformed their instruction manual (a scroll of priestly regulations) into
a broader book of law, so that the canonical version of the holiness code would
contain civil laws, such as

> You shall not defraud your neighbor; you shall not steal; you shall
> not keep for yourself the wages of a laborer until morning.
> (Lv 19:17)

To numerous instructions for the temple priests, humanistic elements were added, the most famous of which is this.

> Love your neighbor as yourself: I am Yahweh. (Lv 19:18)

But the addition of civil and humanistic laws to the torah of the temple priests took place after the failed reformation of Josiah, perhaps during the exile period in Babylon. Like the historian who produced DH, the Aaronid scribes used ancient sources to provide a framework for their growing torah. But they went further back in history than the Deuteronomic circle (which started its history with the final speeches of Moses) and explained that Yahweh gave Israel his torah during the wilderness period. It was in reaction to this claim that Jeremiah is reported to have said:

> For in the day that I brought your ancestors out of the land of Egypt, I did not speak to them or command them concerning burnt offerings and sacrifices. (Jer 7:22)

Hayes and Hooker state that one of the reasons why most scholars believe that the Book of the Law discovered in the temple was the Deuteronomic torah is because the Deuteronomic circle produced the history known as DH, which reports the discovery of the Book of the Law in the temple.[5] But this is the same argument advanced by those who support the traditional view. One of the main purposes of DH was to promote the Book of the Law, *sepher hatorah,* the same law scroll given to Joshua at the beginning of DH by Moses the lawgiver (Jos 1:8). Our view is simply that the Book of the Law was the torah of the group that produced the history later known as DH. It is tempting to discuss this subject (which torah was discovered in the temple?) in greater detail, but it is not a temptation to which we can yield in an introductory book such as this. In our notes for this chapter we will reference the chief books that argue the traditional view, that the Book of the Law was indeed a version of Deuteronomy, chapters 12–26.[6]

A Joint Effort of the Royal Priests and the Shechemite Levites

On the positive side we must point out that the reason why Hayes and Hooker were able to put forth their less than popular view (i.e., that the book discovered was an early form of the holiness code) is that they were aware of something that many of us have a tendency to overlook. That fact is that late in the seventh century the official priests of the temple (Zadokites-Aaronid) were in favor of the centralization and standardization of the religious practices of Judah under Jerusalem control, just as the Deuteronomic circle was. The Deuteronomic circle was small and could not have carried out the national reforms alone. And there is no evidence that it had overthrown or surpassed the power of the royal priesthood.

It is possible that there was a meeting of the minds between the royal priesthood and the persuasive Levites, formerly of Shechem. In other words, *the reformation of Josiah was a joint venture of the royal priesthood and the priests and scribes who made up the Deuteronomic circle.* And the foundation for the reformation was found in the introduction to DH, an early version of the book of Deuteronomy.

> This is the law which Moses set before the Israelites. (Dt 4:4)

> Hear O Israel, the LORD is our God, the LORD alone. (Dt 6:4)

> You must demolish completely all the places where the nations …served their gods, on the mountain heights, on the hills, and under every leafy tree. Break down their altars, smash their pillars, burn their sacred poles with fire, and hew down the idols of their gods, and thus blot out their name from their places. (Dt 12:2–3)

What Led to Cooperation Between the Royal Priests and the Shechemites?

During the period of silence we described in chapter 20, there must have been periods of serious communication and interaction between the majority priesthood and the small circle of marginal Levitical priests and scribes that produced DH. Here are some of the things that may have happened between these two parties, leading to the cooperative respect that made a joint effort possible.

(1) The Shechemites, a pro-Yahweh group, gained an appreciation of the role that royal Davidic theology played in preserving and advancing the worship of Yahweh.

(2) The oracles of the great poet-statesman Isaiah played a role in the emergence of Deuteronomistic theology.

(3) The survival of Jerusalem following the failure of Sennacherib to capture and destroy the city made a deep impression on the Shechemites and moved them in the direction of Zion theology.

(4) Some of the priests of the temple were scholars and were appreciative of the value of learning Shechemite traditions.

(5) The royal priesthood was impressed by the value the Shechemites placed on the recording of the oracles of Amos and Hosea and later Isaiah and Micah. The Shechemites may also have started on a framework for their history of Israel and Judah.

(6) The Josian reforms would have strengthened the Jerusalem priesthood and would have been highly profitable for the city of Jerusalem.

(7) During the reign of Josiah, the immense Assyrian empire, which had dominated the Palestine-Syria area for three centuries, began to crumble.

(8) Both priesthoods believed that the promotion of one God for Judah, with the prohibition of foreign (so-called) worship, would have produced one united people, giving Judah a solidarity and nationalistic unity heretofore unknown.

The Failed Reformation and the Split Between the Aaronids and the Deuteronomists

Following the death of Josiah, the reform effort came to a halt. Cooperation between the Deuteronomic circle and the royal priesthood also came to a halt. Basic theological differences between the two priesthoods became obvious as political circumstances changed. Judah immediately became a vassal of Egypt. Jehoiakim (609–598) was an obedient vassal of Egypt.

> Jehoiakim gave silver and gold to Pharaoh but he taxed the land in order to meet Pharaoh's demand for money. (2 Kgs 23:35)

It is interesting that, after the death of Josiah, there is no further mention of Josiah's reform. We are provided with no afterthoughts or analysis. Whoever completed DH added the post-Josianic period as if there had been no reformation attempt.[7] This fact, coupled with the fact that the reformation as described would have been too sweeping to have been successful, forces us to entertain the thought that the reformation of Josiah as we now have it may be an idealized version of what actually was attempted.[8] And we firmly believe that the Deuteronomic circle and the Deuteronomists who continued the circle's work were skilled in projecting idealizations into Israel's past. For the authors of DH, it was back to the drawing board.

The Masses of Judah

It is interesting to note that in our previous list concerning the many elements that made up the description of Josiah's reign, the reaction of the people of Judah, the masses of average Judahites, was not included. We are not given a hint concerning the popularity of the reformation or the opposition that may have come from the people.

While it is important for students of the bible to understand the theological tension between the Aaronids and the Levites, we must inform ourselves that the people of Judah had no interest in or understanding of the theological debate that would continue for two centuries. The people continued to worship at multiple high places, burn incense to other gods, and participate in fertility rites, erecting pillars *(massebim)* and poles *(asherim),* serving and using idols. Both priests and independent mediums assisted farmers and others in determining the will of (or influencing) an assortment of unnamed gods. Blessings were sought for loved ones and curses for enemies. Activities were engaged in to honor and communicate with the dead. Peasants sought after and used the services of wizards, necromancers, soothsayers, local holy persons, and so forth. Activities at household shrines differed greatly. Were the truth to be known, very few people outside of Jerusalem knew or cared about the dispute between the royal priests and the Levites of Shechem.

However, in the canonical Hebrew bible the Josianic reformation attempt was described as thorough. At the top of the effort, in the temple, all gods were to be banned except Yahweh. The attributes of El had already been absorbed by Yahweh, and an attempt was made to eliminate the worship of Baal and Asherah. All foreign worship was to be banned in Jerusalem. Throughout Judah high places that traced their origin back for centuries were to be eliminated. Only by these drastic measures could the goals of the reform as recorded be reached. Religious practices customary in rural areas and limited to the family were also included in the reform.[9]

So What Really Happened?

We believe in the historicity of a sincere reformation movement by Josiah, but it is difficult to believe that it was as extensive as the canonical (final) account would have us believe. There were two phases to the reform effort. It started with the exclusive place for Yahweh in the Jerusalem temple, requiring the elimination of foreign deities and other deities, and needed the elimination of the multiple high places in order to assure complete compliance with the Yahweh-only nature of the effort. But in the nation-state of Judah, there were too many factions, too many vested interests, and too much diversity to believe that a reformation as complete as the one described would have been possible.

But the members of the Deuteronomic circle were determined and creative: it is, thus, reasonable to believe that the description of the Josian movement was idealized after the final destruction of Judah, during the period of the exile. The priests and scribes of the Deuteronomists had nothing to lose by including a description of every change they envisioned as promoting both the uniqueness of Yahweh and the dignity of humans. The assertiveness they demonstrated came from the confidence of knowing that they were the pioneers of a new age, in possession of profound religious concepts based on laws that, in most cases, enhanced the human condition. They were not monotheists, but they recognized the power of the step in the direction of one god for a united people.

NOTES

1. On the other hand, it is possible that there was no summary closing sentence for the Josianic edition (DTR1). The historian may have planned to add to the Josianic edition as further events transpired. Of course, the historian did not foresee the tragic events that transpired following his death. Nor are we given any information concerning the turmoil his death produced. Judah became a vassal of Egypt in one day.

2. The full name of the book is *A New Chronology for the Kings of Israel and Judah and Its Implications for Biblical History and Literature* (Atlanta: John Knox Press), 1988. See pp. 85–88.

3. In this chapter we are using the word *torah* in the narrow sense to mean a collection of laws. The word *Torah* is used in Judaism to identify the first five books of the Bible, the Pentateuch. The *Torah* is the first section of the Tanakh. In the Pentateuch there are four collections of law:
   (1) The Book of the Covenant (Ex 20:22–23:33).
   (2) Holiness Code (Lv 17–26).
   (3) The Priestly Code (scattered throughout the Tetrateuch).
   (4) The Deuteronomic Torah (Dt 12–26).

4. See Susan Ackerman's discussion of holiness in *Under Every Green Tree*, pp. 211–12.

5. See p. 88, Hayes and Hooker, *A New Chronology*.

6. These are four of the chief works to be consulted: Frank Moore Cross, *Canaanite Myth and Hebrew Epic* (Cambridge: Harvard University Press, 1973). Richard Elliot Friedman, *The Exile and Biblical Narrative*, Harvard Semitic Monographs (Chico, Calif.: Scholars Press, 1981). R. D. Nelson, *The Double Redaction of the Deuteronomistic History* (Sheffield, U.K.: JSOT Press, 1981). Andrew D. H. Mayes, *The Story of Israel Between Settlement and Exile* (London: SCM Press, 1983).

7. The one paragraph in the post-Josianic portion of DH that may refer to the reformation is the statement about the sins of Manasseh in 24:3.
   Surely this came upon Judah at the command of the LORD, to remove them out of his sight, for the sins of Manasseh…the LORD was not willing to pardon.
The implication may be that in spite of the righteous attempt of Josiah to please Yahweh, the sins of Manasseh were simply too vile. This may have

been an early attempt by some scribe to account for the destruction of Jerusalem by King Nebuchadnezzar.

8. Historian Gosta W. Ahlstrom doubts the historicity of the Josianic reform and also raises questions concerning the Book of the Law discovered in the temple. See *History of Ancient Palestine*, pp. 773–78.

9. Notice that in setting up the description of the reformation by listing the sins of Manasseh we read:

...he [Manasseh] practiced soothsaying and augury, and dealt with mediums and with wizards. (2 Kgs 21:6)

Part V
ISRAEL AFTER NATIONHOOD
(586–440 B.C.E.)

22

The Royal Priests in Babylon
and the Aaronid Torah[1]

When the Chaldean (neo-Babylonian) armies conquered Judah early in the sixth century, the furthest thing from the collective mind of all parties was the plethora of theological developments that were about to formulate in the religion of the Judahites as a consequence of the defeat and destruction of Jerusalem and the exile of most of its leaders.

People of the Book

We do not have certain knowledge concerning the role scrolls played in preexilic Israel. There is good reason to believe that the scrolls of the Shechemite Levites were produced for public reading to reach didactic goals. We know that the core of the scroll of Amos in its Josianic form is the script for a public liturgy.

Scrolls, which were carried into Babylon and Egypt by the defeated and devastated people of Jerusalem, were read, studied, searched, memorized, and adored by the scattered communities during the captivity period.[2] They were also edited and emended, and several important ancient scrolls were artistically blended together to produce new scrolls that would give an entirely new religious identity to Israel. The Aaronid priests contributed their part to what would become the canonical bible, beginning their production of the Tetrateuch[3] by blending (or using a blended version of) written sources, already ancient, which scholars later called J (for Jahwist, or Yahwist) and E (for Elohim). These sources are referred to as JE and were incorporated into the priestly structure found presently in the first four books of the bible.

A popularly held belief is that the central place of writings recognized as scripture by Judahites first developed during the Babylonian captivity among the exilic community in Babylon, a community wrenched from its homeland, deprived of its reigning king, the temple of its God, and the sacred city of its God's choosing. It is probably true that a new, unprecedented level of literacy was reached by this group, preparing the way for the designation that would later be applied to Judaism, People of the Book.

Our premise is that scrolls that later found their way into the canonical scriptures were produced by schools with important theological differences. It is important to keep in mind that following the destruction of Jerusalem, there were at least three Judahite communities. Persons associated with the apparatus of the monarchy, political leaders, and royal priests found themselves in Babylon. But there were at least two other significant Judahite communities. One of these communities was in Egypt, and the other community, poor and without status, was in Judah, amidst and near the ruins of Jerusalem. Literacy may not have increased among the persons left behind, not taken into captivity. They expended all their energy on survival concerns, and religious leadership skills had exited the land to Babylon or to Egypt.

Of the three communities mentioned above, there has always been an emphasis on the Babylonian community (to the exclusion of the other two). The vitality of this bias lies in the attractiveness it contains. It is inspiring to picture the devastated, humiliated people of Judah in Babylonian captivity, surrounded by Babylonian pomposity, searching their writings and enlarging them, knowing as we do the role these writings would play in the history of their descendants and the totality of western civilization for millennia.

> By the rivers of Babylon—
> there we sat down and there we wept
> when we remembered Zion.
> …If I forget you O Jerusalem,
> let my right hand wither!
> Let my tongue cleave to the roof of my mouth,
> if I do not remember you,
> If I do not set Jerusalem above my highest joy.
> (Ps 137:1, 5–6)

Judahites remaining in Judah were equally devastated in spite of the fact that they were not relocated. To complete our picture of scattered Israel, we must not forget the community of Judahites in Egypt. Jeremiah and Baruch were among their number. In order to understand the development of the theologies of ancient Israel and the growth of updated scrolls into the canonical version of the Hebrew bible, the word of God, we have to be aware of the interaction of at least these three groups: (a) the Babylonian Judahite community; (b) Judahites left behind in the land and never carried away as captives of war; (c) and the small but very influential community in Egypt that produced the enlarged, emended edition of the Deuteronomistic history, the eighth-century prophets, and the scroll of Jeremiah—a collection that became the very heart of the Hebrew bible.[4] In the chapter on the Persian period, we will discuss the Judahites who remained in Judah during the captivity period.

The Split Between the Aaronids and Levites

In the previous chapter we suggested that the reformation of Josiah fell short of its goals with his untimely death. Whoever continued DH to its present conclusion did not discuss the reformation of Josiah, analyze it, or even mention it. As a matter of fact, the editor/author of the concluding chapters of 2 Kings ignored both Hezekiah and Josiah when he wrote these words about Jehoiakim:

> He did what was evil in the sight of the LORD, just as all his fathers had done. (2 Kgs 23:37)

Considering that Josiah was the father of Jehoiakim, the phrase does not seem to be very thoughtful.

As a result of the reformation, some increased centralization did take place. But in the rural areas, at multiple high places, diversity continued as the norm. Nevertheless, something of great significance was accomplished by the reformation attempt. The understanding of the increased centrality of Yahweh as the high God of Judah by the Aaronid-royal priesthood, moving in the direction of the Deuteronomic circle of Levites, became the platform on which changing theologies would be built. After Josiah's death, because of the subjection of the house of David to the rule of Egypt, followed shortly by the invasion of Judah by the neo-Babylonians, the royal priesthood recognized the necessity and value of the unique role of Yahweh in the nation's future.

We stated in chapter 21 that following Josiah's death, the two priesthoods that had cooperated in supporting the reformation separated because of theological differences. Each held a perception of Yahweh that was virtually incompatible with the other's views. We turn now to the Aaronid priesthood in Babylon.

The Aaronid Priests in Babylonian Captivity

Before the exile, the royal priests conceived of Yahweh as preoccupied with animal sacrifices, other temple sacrifices, priestly procedures, and ritual uncleanness. For them the glory *(kabod)* of Yahweh filled the temple as a sign of his presence. In Psalm 135, an Aaronid Psalm, Yahweh was said to dwell in Jerusalem.[5]

> O house of Israel, bless the LORD!
> O house of Aaron, bless the LORD!
> ...Blessed be the LORD from Zion, he who resides
> in Jerusalem. (Ps 135:20–21)

Some members of the Aaronid priesthood in Babylon were able to organize themselves—after a period of time passed, of course—and to take action to meet newly emerging goals. The first of these goals was to assist the Judahite community to maintain its identity in captivity. As time passed, there was the real possibility that the children of former Judahites would become comfortable, and even prosperous, in their new homes, close to the center of world power.[6] For this reason the formerly royal priests sought to establish a role for themselves within the Judahite community in the light of two possible futures: (a) one without a return to Jerusalem or a new beginning for the destroyed temple, or (b) one that included a return to Jerusalem and the possible reconstruction of the former temple. There are some scholars who believe that the beautiful poetry of Second Isaiah was written to persuade second and third generation Judahites in captivity to return to Jerusalem.[7]

With this background information we are able to see the strategy that guided the development of the Aaronid torah. Consider the following: (1) Because the total number of Judahites in Babylon was relatively small (not large enough to support a formerly royal priesthood), deportees were encouraged to be fruitful and multiply.[8] (2) Whatever the status of sabbath observance during the last days of the nation-state of Judah, weekly sabbath observance became a central and key religious practice of the Babylonian community.[9] Sabbath observance was built into the priestly creation account and the priestly version of the ten commandments in Exodus 20:11.

> For in six days the LORD made heaven and earth, the sea, and all
> that is in them, but rested on the seventh day.[10]

(3) Adding to the preservation of Judahite identity was the insistence by the priests on circumcision for all male babies on their eighth day.[11]

(4) As a result of witnessing the splendor and pageantry of Babylonian worship, the royal priests recognized the importance of beautiful, meaningful robes and garments for the proper priesthood and incorporated the many requirements for priestly attire that we now find in the Tetrateuch.[12]

> Then bring near to you your brother Aaron, and his sons with him,
> to serve me as priests....When they make these sacred vestments
> for your brother Aaron and his sons to serve me as priests, they
> shall use gold, blue, purple, and crimson yarns, and fine linen.
> (Ex 28:1, 4–5)

(5) Insistence on observation of strict dietary laws would certainly contribute to a strong sense of identity for deportees in a foreign country. We cannot say for sure what the status of the dietary laws was in monarchical Judah. Many of the laws may have developed originally as practices of health, but by the time they reached the torah, they were part of the priestly program of holiness (ceremonial cleanness) at all costs.[13] (6) A new national holy day was introduced by the Aaronids, the Day of Atonement (Lv 16). A Day of Atonement *(yom kippur)* is unknown in Deuteronomy. (7) A new literary version of the exodus was produced, and fathers were expected to teach their children the details of this literary version of the exodus experience.[14]

As we can see above, much of the Tetrateuch becomes intelligible to us when we consider the role played by the Aaronid priests in the setting of Babylonian captivity. The use of ancient sources, such as J and E placed in the priestly literary structure, informs us how the Aaronids viewed the people of Yahweh and their role (i.e., the priests') in the life of a newly emerging Jewish culture.[15]

We stated that our belief was that the royal priests were first impressed with the use and function of written scrolls for the education of the people of Judah when the Shechemite Levites arrived in Jerusalem following the fall of the northern kingdom.[16] Before that time the Aaronid scrolls were primarily private priestly manuals for the guidance of the priests alone. This characteristic is evident throughout the Tetrateuch and makes parts of Exodus, Numbers, and Leviticus very difficult reading for the modern student.

Animal Sacrifices

Since so much of the Aaronid torah deals with animal sacrifices (for example, Leviticus chapter 1 and chapters 3 to 7 and many others), we should clarify our view concerning this practice. When the Aaronids went to Babylon, they took with them a manual they had produced containing regulations and procedures concerning animal sacrifices at the Jerusalem temple. After several decades they regained their balance in captivity and expanded their torah to include explicit laws concerning subjects that would reenforce the identity of Judahites in Babylon as the people of Yahweh. These subjects have been discussed above and include circumcision, sabbath observance, *yom kippur,* dietary laws, and so forth. At the same time the scribes may have expanded the laws concerning animal sacrifices. Since we know very little about the sacrificial procedures in monarchical Israel, we have to rely on these writings, which may have been idealized during captivity to enhance the need for animal sacrifices and make the procedures more in accordance with priestly beliefs and expectations.

Why would the royal priests do this? Because they had hopes of eventually reinstating the animal sacrificial system either in Babylon at a tent shrine or in a rebuilt Jerusalem if the opportunity to return and rebuild Jerusalem became a reality. Profane slaughter was eliminated, and all animal slaughter became a sacrifice. The conclusion was that if you did not sacrifice your animal to Yahweh, you sacrificed your animal to some other god.

Animal sacrifices were a natural thing for a country largely composed of farming families. Once institutionalized by the royal priests, the procedures would continue to survive, especially in the capital city at the national temple. We have no information concerning the procedures of animal sacrifices at the high places, but there are scattered references to animal sacrifice in books containing narrative accounts, such as Genesis, Exodus, and DH. And this brings us to the complicated instructions for the tent shrine that the priests envisioned.

The Tent Shrine

The chronology presented in the canonical scriptures confronts the reader with an idealized picture of an ancient community of Israelites, a valuable theological reconstruction that has no basis in history. If you remember our opening chapters of this short history, Israel first emerged in the highlands of Canaan as a nation of subsistence farmers during the last decades of the thirteenth century. This historical Israel did not spend forty years in the wilderness after a miraculous deliverance from Egypt.[17] The question we must answer is, where did the instructions for the building of the tent come from, including dimensions, materials, specifications for furnishings, and so forth (see Ex 26 and Ex 36–38, for example)?

The most logical answer is that the information concerning the tent shrine came from Solomon's temple. And the particularities for Solomon's temple came from Syria and other areas of the ancient Near East. The instructions for the building of the tent shrine in their present form, however, have been worked over by the Aaronid priests in captivity to conform to a priestly vision of the ideal tent shrine, a description of a shrine made in accordance with a wish list. (If you could have everything you wanted in a tent shrine, what would you ask for?)

But why did the priests spend so much energy writing about an ideal tent rather than a permanent building, a temple. The answer is that a tent shrine was envisioned for the Babylonian community of Judahites, a shrine that could be taken apart and carried by the people of Judah back to Jerusalem if and when the opportunity presented itself. A rebuilt temple in Jerusalem remained a future hope, but they needed a shrine that would do for the time being. The shrine of the Aaronid torah was a portable shrine. In the canonical wilderness tradition, the Levites would take down the shrine when it was time for Israel to move on.[18]

Contribution of the Priestly School

In recent times, as a result of groundbreaking work in form, source, and redaction criticism, first on the part of German scholars and later by Scandinavian, Dutch, American, and other scholars, the literary contribution of the royal priests in exile has been negatively evaluated. When it was determined that the priestly writings were largely exilic and did not predate the Deuteronomistic school or share the Deuteronomistic theology, scholars began to accuse the priestly school of rewriting Israelite history, placing too much emphasis on animal sacrifice and other temple activity, insuring their own power over Levitical priests, and not paying enough attention to humanistic matters pertaining to social justice.

It is our view that it is wiser to be more appreciative of the priestly school and its contribution. While it is true that the priests rewrote the history of early Israel, we remember that the Deuteronomists also rewrote the history of Israel, even though DH started at a later time after the wilderness experience. There was nothing new in projecting theology into Israel's past. And there was nothing unusual for a priesthood to establish and expand its own legitimacy. The Deuteronomists also had vested interests and as a group traced their ancestry to a Shechemite priesthood that began to direct its venom toward the monarchy of the northern kingdom after rejection by the first king, Jeroboam I.

As far as justice issues go, we do feel that the Deuteronomic circle was far ahead of the Aaronids in its social agenda. But when the priests began to expand their priestly manual to become the temple torah, they included statements related to human relations in society. It is in the priestly source that we read:

> You shall not deal falsely; and you shall not lie to one another....You shall not defraud your neighbor....You shall not revile the deaf or put a stumbling block before the blind....You shall not render an unjust judgement....You shall not hate in your heart anyone of your kin....You shall love your neighbor as yourself: I am the LORD. (Lv 19:11–17)

The Day of Atonement *(yom kippur),* which the priests conceived of and initiated, has proven its value and functionality by enduring in Judaism for more than twenty-four hundred years. The priestly emphasis on ritual, liturgy, vestments, and strict observance of holy days has greatly enriched the culture of Western civilization and has played a vital role in the practices of many leading branches of the Christian Church. In many Protestant churches there has been a rediscovery of the importance of ritual, vestments, ceremony, and pageantry in the nature and practice of worship. And we cannot forget the glorious tone poem that opens the Hebrew bible with the creation of the heavens and the earth. The priests were able to divorce this magnificent account from Babylonian and Ugaritic myth and legend to produce a brilliant theological statement. If the only product of the Aaronid priests was the creation account, the world would still be deeply indebted to them.

NOTES

1. In the next two chapters we will be referring to the two torahs (*toroth*) of the two major priesthoods, the Aaronids and the Levites. We are using the word *torah* to mean a collection of laws received from God. The torah of the Aaronids is found in parts of Exodus, Leviticus, and Numbers. We call the priests Aaronids because the royal priests distinguished themselves from Levites by stating that they were descended from Aaron. Please note that the name Aaron appears sixty times in the book of Leviticus, ninety-five times in the book of Numbers, and only four times in the book of Deuteronomy. The torah of the Aaronids is sometimes broken into two sections with two titles, the holiness code, Leviticus 17–26, and the priestly code, referring to laws, rules, and regulations appearing throughout Exodus, Leviticus, and Numbers, sometimes including the holiness code.

2. See Andrew Dearman, *Religion and Culture in Ancient Israel* (Peabody, Mass.: Hendrickson, 1992), pp. 100–101.

3. The Tetrateuch consists of the first four books of the Hebrew bible. These books, because they propose to explain what took place before the speeches of Moses in Deuteronomy, are located before Deuteronomy even though Deuteronomy was a scroll of the Levites before the Tetrateuch was constructed. The first three chapters of Deuteronomy now serve as a bridge between the Tetrateuch and the scrolls of the Deuteronomists. For a discussion of the priestly source (P), we recommend Norman Gottwald's book *The Hebrew Bible: A Socio-literary Introduction*, pp. 469–82. This is section 49 and is titled "Rounding Out the Law: The Priestly Writer."

4. Robert and Mary Coote, in their book *Power, Politics, and the Making of the Bible*, speak of changes made to DH by the priestly scribes of the court and in Babylonian captivity, and the authors even call DTR2 Jehoiachin's revision (pp. 70–71). However, a page later they write that the Deuteronomistic history (DH) was not suitable for revision, as it was in the hands of Levitical interests and spoke Levitical prerogatives (p. 72). The position we are taking in this book is that the royal priests emended their own torah (the holiness code) and the Deuteronomists in Egypt revised DTR1. The revisions to DTR1 completely changed certain theological perspectives of DH. The most significant revision was concerned with the extended metaphor of the vassal treaty form, which is generally referred to by scholars as covenant theology.

5. The Levites did not share these views of Yahweh's concerns. For one thing Yahweh did not dwell in Jerusalem. Jerusalem was the place chosen by Yahweh for *his name to dwell.*

6. In the early years of the captivity, Jeremiah had written a letter to the captives telling them to settle down and make Babylon their home, raising their families and seeking the welfare of the city where they found themselves (Jer 29:1–14). Jeremiah assumed that the Judahites would be anxious to return to Jerusalem after seventy years, but that was not the case for many families of the deportees.

7. See the Cootes' book *Power, Politics, and the Making of the Bible*, p. 71.

8. The expression "be fruitful and multiply" is one that identifies the priestly source. These are the first words of God to man and woman after their creation in Genesis 1:28.

9. An interesting reference can be found in the book of Amos concerning sabbath observance. Amos, speaking of exploitation by merchants, ties the sabbath with the month rather than the week.

> Hear this you that trample on the needy
> …saying, "When will the new moon be over so
> that we may sell grain,
>   and the sabbath,
> so that we may offer wheat for sale?" (Am 8:5)

10. There was no reference to creation in six days in the earlier Deuteronomic version of the fourth commandment (Dt 5:12–15).

11. In Deuteronomy circumcision is not required. There circumcision is spiritualized.

> Circumcise, then, the foreskin of your heart. (Dt 10:16)

12. Read the entire twenty-eighth chapter and thirty-ninth chapter of Exodus.

13. The principle behind the dietary laws is explained thoroughly from the Aaronid viewpoint in several places in the Tetrateuch, including Leviticus 11:24–47. This explanation is not found in the oldest collection of laws, the so-called Book of the Covenant (Ex 20:22–23:19). The principle does appear in Deuteronomy 14:3–21. A. D. H. Mayes states that the Deuteronomic passage has been extended by an editor influenced by the Leviticus passage. See Mayes, *The New Century Bible Commentary: Deuteronomy*, pp. 239–43.

14. What role the exodus played in Jerusalem theology before the exile

is not certain. For example, looking back, we see that the exodus was not important to Isaiah of Jerusalem.

15. There are some scholars who believe that P was completed before it was blended with PJE. Our suggestion is that P in its earliest form was a priestly manual, not a public document. It reached one level of development during the reign of Hezekiah but in rudimentary form existed even earlier. The Aaronid learned from the Shechemites the value of *public* scrolls for purposes of popular education.

16. We cannot say for sure that the royal priests first recognized the importance of the use of scrolls for the education of the people as a result of the Shechemite practices of scroll production for this purpose. Perhaps the concept would have emerged during the last days of the monarchy because it was a concept whose time had come. We maintain that the Levites were ahead of the royal priests in this area. During the captivity there certainly was time to reorganize for the needs of exiled Judahites, and scroll creation and expansion definitely took place.

17. As Martin Noth and many other scholars have demonstrated in many writings, traditions that now compose the Tetrateuch were separate traditions that have been knit together. These include exodus, wilderness, and Sinai traditions. Any one of these could have been part of the traditions of a group—or several groups—that joined the historical Israel early, in the days before the monarchy. These traditions grew during the monarchy and appeared in the J source and the E source and may also have existed in other sources, both oral and written, throughout the rural areas of Israel and Judah. In their present form they are entirely theologized.

18. See Exodus 40:36, Numbers 2, and Numbers 9:15–23.

23

The Invention of the Prophetic Class

While the royal priests in Babylon were creating a strong religious identity for Judahites in captivity, a group of Levite scribes and priests in Egypt were dealing with another problem.[1] The Deuteronomists, as this group would become known much, much later,[2] were searching for answers to questions raised first by the death of Josiah and later by the destruction of Jerusalem and the temple.

Theologically, one of several things had happened to the nation of Judah. (1) Yahweh had not kept his promise to the house of David that it would endure forever; or (2) Yahweh was not as strong as the gods of the Babylonians who opposed him; or (3) if Yahweh had not kept his promise, why not?

In the Josianic version of DH (the version of the Deuteronomic history that appeared during the reign of Josiah), the behavior of the monarchs had decided the fate of the nation. Yahweh had destroyed Israel because the kings of Israel had followed in the sin of Jeroboam, Israel's first king. For example, we read of Baasha:

> He [Baasha] did what was evil in the sight of the LORD, walking in the way of Jeroboam and in the sin that he caused Israel to commit. (1 Kgs 15:34)

The northern kingdom had not had a chance; all the kings were evil. But Judah had been a different story. Yahweh's covenant with David, like God's covenant with Abraham of Hebron, was without conditions and eternal. God promised land and progeny.

> He [David's son] shall build a house for my name, and I will establish the throne of his [David's] kingdom forever....I will not take my steadfast love from him, as I took it from Saul....Your

173

> house and your kingdom shall be made sure forever before me;
> your throne shall be established forever. (2 Sm 7:13–16)

But perhaps *forever* didn't really mean forever and under *any* conditions. The kings of Judah had worshiped and served other gods and did not remain true to Yahweh. One of the purposes of DH was to show that the kings of Judah were unable to live up to Yahweh's expectations because the Book of the Law had been lost for centuries. When the Book of the Law was discovered in the temple during the reign of Josiah, Josiah immediately repented and instigated a massive reformation, the results of which would make the heart of Yahweh rejoice. Then why did Josiah's reform fail, and why did Yahweh allow Josiah to die in battle?

A new ending was added to the Josianic edition of DH, one that provided an early and unsatisfactory answer. Manasseh was blamed for the destruction of Judah.

> Still the LORD did not turn from the fierceness of his great wrath,
> by which his anger was kindled against Judah, because of all the
> provocations with which Manasseh had provoked him. The LORD
> said "I will remove Judah also out of my sight....I will reject this
> city which I have chosen, Jerusalem, and the house of which I said
> 'My name shall be there.'" (2 Kgs 23:26–27)

After some time passed, the theological heirs of the Deuteronomic circle, dissatisfied with the superficiality of the answer that blamed everything on Manasseh, came up with a comprehensive answer for the questions raised by the failure of the reformation and the ultimate destruction of Jerusalem and the temple. Influenced by the elements of the vassal treaty form (with which Judah had been ruled by three major military powers, Assyria, Egypt, and Babylon), the Deuteronomists changed the meaning of the word *covenant (brith)* forever.

The Meaning of the Word *Covenant*

The word *covenant* is a theological word that has acquired a tremendously heavy structure. For a thousand years before the exile, the Hebrew word for "covenant" had nothing whatever to do with the vassal treaty form. The Hebrew word is built on three consonants, *BRT,* and means "agreement," "arrangement between two or several parties," "treaty," "contract," "bargain," or "obligation." It appears in English transliteration in various forms: *berit, berith, brith,* and *beyrith.* The letters *BRT* form the root of a noun.[3]

The word *covenant* is used to describe a great variety of relationships. Here are three examples:

I will make for you a covenant on that day with the wild animals, the birds of the air, and the creeping things of the ground. (Hos 2:18)[4]

They did not remember the covenant of kinship. (Am 1:9)

We have made a covenant with death, and with Sheol we have an agreement. (Is 28:15)

In the Josianic edition of DH, the word *berith* is used in a wide variety of ways. Often the parties are identified. Here are three examples:

Jonathan made a covenant with David because he loved him. (1 Sm 18:3)

...and all the men of Jabesh said to Nahash, "Make a covenant [treaty] with us and we will serve you." (1 Sm 11:1)

But in the seventh year Jehoiada summoned the captains of the Carites and of the guards and had them come to him in the house of the LORD. He made a covenant with them and put them under an oath in the house of the LORD. (2 Kgs 11:4)

One meaning the word *brith* did not have in the Josianic version was the structured meaning based on the vassal treaty form.

The Use of Metaphor by the Deuteronomists

In seeking to describe Israel, Israel's God, and the relationship between Israel and its God, the Deuteronomists of both the Josianic period and the exile made generous use of metaphor. They may have learned the use of metaphor from the scroll of Hosea. In the original oracles of Hosea, as identified by Gale Yee in her dissertation, *Composition and Tradition in the Book of Hosea: A Redactional Critical Investigation,*[5] twelve metaphors were used to describe Israel. They were all negative. Before the scroll of Hosea reached its final form, it contained twenty-seven metaphors for Israel, nine added by the exilic editor of Hosea.[6] It also contained a series of metaphors for Yahweh.

The Deuteronomists learned to use many metaphors to describe the relationship between Israel and Yahweh. Three popular metaphors were parent and child (Hos 11:1), husband and wife (Hos 2:19), and protector and vassal (Is 31:45).

The Metaphor of the Vassal Treaty Form

Following the devastation of Judah, when a profound and satisfactory answer to the question "Why had the LORD visited this severe punishment on his people?" was desperately needed, the extended and complete development of the vassal treaty metaphor provided the answer. A new understanding of the word *covenant* based on the ancient Near Eastern vassal treaty form provided a complete reinterpretation of Israel's history by the exilic heirs of the Deuteronomic circle to explain the ultimate destruction of Jerusalem and the temple of Yahweh in 586 B.C.E.

The Josianic version of DH was emended and revised along with the scroll of Deuteronomy to reinterpret the history of Israel as a conditional relationship, not between Yahweh and the king, but between Yahweh and the people. It was the disobedience of the people that caused the destruction of Judah and not the evil of the monarchs. So we now read in exilic portions of DH such words as

> They [the people] rejected all the commandments of their God,
> and made for themselves cast images of two calves. (2 Kgs 17:16)

In the Josianic version of DH, the first king of Israel, Jeroboam, was blamed for making the images of the two calves. In the exilic version the people were blamed directly.

In addition to updating DH, the Deuteronomists also provided a new beginning and a new ending for the growing scroll of Deuteronomy.[7] Chapter 4 was the new beginning, and chapters 28 through 30 constituted the new ending.[8]

But there was another problem created by the reinterpretation of Israel's history in accordance with the extended metaphor based on the vassal treaty form. The scroll containing the statutes and ordinances, the very stipulations of the ancient covenant between Yahweh and Israel, had not been available to the people. The scroll said to be read by Joshua himself *(sepher hatorah)* was never mentioned after Joshua for the entire course of DH, which emphatically states that the scroll was discovered in the temple only in the reign of Josiah, one of the last kings of Israel. How could the people be held responsible? In order for a vassal relationship to be valid, the vassal has to understand the stipulations, the expectations of the suzerain. The answer to this problem was solved by the Deuteronomists with the invention of a Yahwistic prophetic class.

A Reinterpretation of the Role of Saints, Poets, and Orators in the History of Israel

There had never been a clear-cut prophetic class in Israel or Judah speaking for Yahweh. There had been poets, saints, angry spokespersons, holy men and women, and others recognized for their fervor and zeal who may or may have not spoken of or for Yahweh. But the Deuteronomists of the exile created a prophetic class of persons who spoke to Israel/Judah for Yahweh *throughout the history of the nation,* informing the masses of Yahweh's laws, statutes, ordinances, and requirements, his concern for cultic purity, and so forth.

The Yahwistic prophets as an ongoing institution are established by Deuteronomistic statements found in Jeremiah, Amos, Hosea, and DH. During the exile this defining statement appeared in the scroll of Jeremiah.

> From the day that your ancestors came out of the land of Egypt until this day, I persistently sent all my servants the prophets to them, day after day; yet they did not listen to me or pay attention. (Jer 7:25)[9]

Notice the phrase *my servants the prophets.* It is an exilic phrase. A variation of this phrase was added to the canonical scroll of Amos.

> Surely the LORD does nothing without revealing his secret to his servants the prophets. (Am 3:7)

The phrase appears again in an explanation as to why the northern kingdom was destroyed.

> Yet the LORD warned Israel and Judah, saying "Turn from your evil ways and keep my commandments and my statutes, in accordance with all the law that I commanded your ancestors and that I sent to you by my servants the prophets. They would not listen but were stubborn, as their ancestors had been." (2 Kgs 17:13–14)[10]

An exilic sentence in Hosea reads:

> I [the LORD] spoke to the prophets;
> It was I who multiplied visions,
> and through the prophets I will bring destruction.
> (Hos 12:10)[11]

The Literary Prophets

The Deuteronomists created a prophetic history that was not in accord with the facts. Before the period of the exile, there were only four literary prophets whose oracles have been preserved for us, Amos, Hosea, Isaiah, and Micah. Their original oracles were not concerned with the people's disregard for the statutes and ordinances of Yahweh. Amos addressed his angry words to the decision makers of Samaria because they oppressed the masses, but Amos called the farmers of Israel the righteous (Am 2:6 and 5:12). In one Amos tradition Amos denied being a *nabi*. *Nabi* became the Deuteronomists' favorite word for a prophet. Isaiah was the state poet of Judah during the reign of Ahaz. Isaiah was primarily concerned with the house of David, the royal theology, and affairs of state. Long passages in Isaiah that condemn the sins of the inhabitants of Judah and Israel are Deuteronomic/Deuteronomistic additions to the scroll that carries his name (chapter 1, for example). For the first thirty-five chapters of Isaiah, he is not called a *nabi*. It is only in the Deuteronomic passages of the Hezekiah narrative that Isaiah is referred to as a *nabi*. Negative passages concerning prophets appear in Isaiah. Prophets of Israel are called "…prophets who teach lies." In another negative remark we read:

> …he [the LORD] has closed your eyes, you prophets, and covered your heads, you seers. (Is 29:10)

Hosea was primarily concerned with the relationship between the power structure of Samaria and the military/political alliances they made with Egypt and Assyria. Passages in Hosea that condemn the people of Israel for failure to keep the statutes and ordinances of Yahweh are Josianic or exilic additions to his scroll. Gale Yee, in her definitive study of Hosea, identifies passages like the following as exilic.[12]

> The people of Israel…they turn to other gods and
>   love raisin cakes. (Hos 3:1)
> …the men themselves go aside with whores and
>   sacrifice with temple prostitutes. (4:14)
> With their silver and gold they made idols for
>   their own destruction. (8:4)

Oracles that condemn the people are not original Hosea oracles. Other passages that condemn the inhabitants of the land are identified by Gale Yee as the work of the Josianic redactor (Hos 4:1–2, for example).

When Were the Four Eighth-Century Prophets First Called Prophets?

In an original oracle of Hosea he accused the prophets *(nabiim)* of stumbling at night (because of drunkenness, 4:5b). So Amos denied being a prophet, Isaiah was not called a prophet until the Hezekian narrative, and Hosea was primarily a political critic. What about Micah, who like Amos identified with the exploited rural people of his nation? Micah was not given the title prophet. In the title of his scroll, he is simply identified as Micah of Moresheth, and in the scroll of Jeremiah a century later, he is called "the Moreshite." It is our suggestion that the four eighth-century prophets were not considered prophets until the period of the exile. In the Josianic versions of all four redacted scrolls, there were negative passages concerning prophets.[13]

The Nonliterary Prophets

So if the four literary prophets did not demonstrably declare to the people the importance and necessity of keeping the statutes and ordinances of a divinely revealed law code (before exilic redaction), what about the nonliterary prophets like Samuel, Ahijah, Nathan, Gad, Jehu ben Hanani, Elijah, Micaiah, Elisha, and other unnamed prophets? We have identified some of the major nonliterary prophets in the previous sentence, and every one of them had at least one encounter with a king. In chart 8 in chapter 9, we suggested that a conversation between a prophet and a king was a literary convention developed by the Josianic historian. Even if every encounter was a historical fact, there is not one instance of a nonliterary prophet addressing the masses of the people, reminding them or teaching them about the statutes and ordinances of Yahweh's law code, with the possible exception of Samuel and Elijah. In the case of Samuel, who was a combination judge-priest-prophet, in his closing address to the people, he mentions the *commandment of the LORD,* but he may be referring to the demand of the people for a monarch and not a written code of law. In the case of Elijah, Elijah is said to have challenged the people of Israel to choose between Yahweh and the Tyrian Baal, and in his encounter with Ahab in the vineyard of Naboth, he was pictured as a Deuteronomistic prophet concerned with law. In the Naboth incident Elijah did not speak to the people, however. In chapter 14 we stated the reasons for our belief that the Elijah cycle became a part of DH during or after the exile and suggested that the material was heavily redacted (see chart 11).

Our conclusion, after a review of both literary and nonliterary prophets, is that there are no clear-cut examples of any prophet warning the people of the consequences of ignoring the statues and ordinances of Yahweh. Warnings of this nature, when they appear in the prophetic books, are the work of an exilic redactor.

The exilic Deuteronomists were so successful in projecting into Israel's past a prophetic class that constantly taught the people about the stipulations of the covenant, the legal requirements of Yahweh's law, that a century after the exile (450–400 B.C.E.) the chronicler repeated the concept.

...he sent prophets among them to bring them back to the LORD; they testified against them, but they would not listen. (2 Chr 24:19)

> The LORD...sent persistently to them by his messengers...; but they kept mocking the messengers of God, despising his words, and scoffing at his prophets. (2 Chr 36:15–16)

Both the scrolls of Ezra and Nehemiah incorporate the concept of an ongoing prophetic class. In a prayer attributed to Ezra we read:

> For we have forsaken your commandments which you commanded by your servants the prophets. (Ezr 9:11)[14]

And Nehemiah is reported to have said:

> Nevertheless they [the people] were disobedient and rebelled against you and cast your law behind their backs and killed your prophets. (Neh 9:26)

It is interesting to notice the development of a tradition in the above references. In the sixth century the Deuteronomists said the people would not listen to the prophets. In Chronicles it says that the people mocked the messengers and scoffed (2 Chr 36:15). In Ezra the people actually killed the prophets.[15]

Summary

(1) The prophetic class called "my servants the prophets" was an exilic invention of the Deuteronomists in exile.

DEVELOPMENT OF A PROPHETIC TRADITION

Deteriorating Treatment of Prophets in Subsequent Reporting

CHART 15

1. In DH the people would not listen to the prophets and were stubborn (2 Kgs 17:13–14; see also Jer 7:25).

2. In Chronicles it is reported that the people mocked the messengers, despised their words, and scoffed at the prophets (2 Chr 36:15–16).

3. In Nehemiah it is stated that the people cast Yahweh's law behind their back and *killed the prophets* (Neh 9:26).

4. In the New Testament it is reported that the people stoned or murdered the prophets (Mt 21:35 and 23:31 and 37; see also Luke 13:34).

---

(2) The four eighth-century prophets were not considered prophets until after their deaths. In the Josianic version of the so-called eighth-century prophets, prophets *(nabiim)* are looked upon negatively. Micah is not called a *nabi* but is referred to as Micah of Moresheth (Mi 1:1 and Jer 26:18). Isaiah is not called a *nabi* until the Hezekian narrative (chapters 36–39). Amos denied being a *nabi*, and Hosea was a political critic who criticized the prophets of Israel.[16]

(3) The nonliterary prophets like Nathan, Gad, Ahijah, Micaiah, although functional, served literary and theological purposes of the historian and are otherwise obscure.

(4) At any rate, neither the literary prophets nor the nonliterary prophets addressed the people, other than Elijah, whose cycle was redacted by a Deuteronomist (see chapter 14).

(5) The exilic Deuteronomists needed a prophetic class that continually kept the people reminded of the statutes, ordinances, and laws of Yahweh for centuries. So they inserted phrases like

> Yet the LORD warned Israel and Judah, saying "Turn from your evil ways and keep my commandments and my statutes, in accordance with all the law that I commanded your ancestors and that I sent to you by my servants the prophets. They [the people] would not listen but were stubborn, as their ancestors had been." (2 Kgs 17:13–14)

(6) Moses the lawgiver was also made a prophet by the Deuteronomists. (Just another step in the development of the book of Deuteronomy.) Gale Yee identifies the Hosean passages that name Moses as a prophet as exilic (R2).

Why did the Deuteronomists invent a prophetic class? Because the people had to be knowledgeable about the statutes, ordinances, and laws in order to be held responsible for not keeping the stipulations of the vassal-treaty-based covenant metaphor that the Deuteronomists also invented to establish a basis for an explanation of the final destruction of Judah in 586.

NOTES

1. There is no agreement among scholars as to the location of the Deuteronomistic school during the exile. It could have been in Babylon, Tahpanhes, Egypt (where Jeremiah, Baruch, and a small number of Judahites were located, as reported in Jer 43 and 44), or somewhere in Judah. Tahpanhes may have been Daphne, a fortified city on a channel of the Nile. The location of the Deuteronomists is not our concern in this chapter, but the development of their theology is.

2. This school would not be called the Deuteronomists until the nineteenth century A.D. The words *Deuteronomy, Deuteronomic circle,* and *Deuteronomists* do not appear in the Hebrew bible.

3. There are a few scattered examples of the use of the word *covenant* as a verb in some English translations. In the KJV in 2 Chronicles 7:18, it says "I covenanted with your father David" but in the NRSV it says, "I made a covenant with your father David."

4. This is the translation of the RSV. In the NRSV the verse reads as follows: "…they multiply falsehood and violence; they make a treaty with Assyria, and oil is carried to Egypt."

5. Gale Yee, *Composition and Tradition in the Book of Hosea: A Redactional Critical Investigation* (Atlanta: Scholars Press, 1987).

6. The exilic editor of Hosea was the same editor (or at least a member of the same circle of scribes) who edited and produced the exilic version of DH.

7. There are two treaty forms referred to by scholars: the Hittite form (second millennium) and the Assyrian form (first millennium). It is beyond the scope of this book to deal with the differences. The treaty form most frequently cited is described by Moshe Weinfeld in his book *Deuteronomy and the Deuteronomic School*, pp. 59–146. It is the treaty of the Assyrian king Esarhaddon (681–669 B.C.E.), predecessor of Asherbanipal. The student is also referred to a description of the ancient vassal treaty and its relationship to Deuteronomy in a book by Peter Craigie, *Deuteronomy* (Grand Rapids, Mich.: Eerdmans, 1976), pp. 20–32. While Craigie's book takes a very conservative approach, the explanation of the vassal treaty form is valuable for its clarity.

8. In my book *Obsession with Justice: The Story of the Deuteronomists*, I explain how the book of Deuteronomy grew from the center out, in five stages. Notice the vassal treaty language found in chapter 4 (v. 4, v. 9, v. 26, vv. 37–40, to cite a few examples). In chapter 29 we find the oath taken by the vassal (vv. 10–20) and reference to the curses (vv. 20–29). The curses are spelled out in chapters 27 and 28. In the vassal treaty of Esarhaddon with Judah there were more than seventy-five curses listed for the vassal that would break the treaty.

9. See also Jeremiah 44:4, "Yet I persistently sent to you all my servants the prophets."

10. There are other passages that refer to the ongoing Yahwistic prophetic concept.

11. Gale Yee, in *Hosea,* calls this passage the work of R2. R2 is the exilic redactor. See p. 317.

12. Yee, *Hosea,* pp. 315–17.

13. Read Hosea 4:5, Amos 7:14, Micah 3:5–11, and Isaiah 29:10.

14. Ezra goes on to connect marriage between the returnees and the inhabitants of the land with uncleanness and pollution, revealing a totally Aaronid interpretation of the prophetic activity. Read verses 10–15.

15. The New Testament continues the tradition of Ezra by stating that the people stoned the prophets (Mt 23:31).

16. H. W. Wolff, in *Interpreting the Prophets,* writes, "In the eighth century, prophets began to appear whose words were addressed to the nation as a whole...." We agree with Wolff that before the eighth century, so-called prophets, including Moses and Samuel, did not address the nation as a whole. But we disagree with the idea that this changed in the eighth century. On the contrary, each one (Amos, Hosea, Isaiah, and Micah) had a limited audience of elite decision makers in the capital cities of Samaria and Jerusalem (Philadelphia: Fortress Press, 1987, p. 14).

24

Judah During the Exile

While the Aaronid royal priests in Babylonian captivity were creating and molding a distinct Judahite identity involving circumcision, sabbath observance, dietary laws, and a vision of a magnificently costumed priesthood with extended duties in a tent shrine, and the Deuteronomists (perhaps in Egypt) were re-creating Israel's past in terms of a vassal-treaty covenant metaphor, what was happening to the majority of the rural Judahites who were never carried away into captivity?

For one thing those who were left behind did not have to be immediately concerned about their identity. Later, when the deportees returned, an identity crisis may be said to have developed, but in the meantime the masses knew they were Judahites. They also knew that Jerusalem had been destroyed by a great political and military power from the distant east, one of those military powers that had been invading and controlling Jerusalem for centuries. While some may have looked on the destruction of Jerusalem and the monarchy indifferently, others looked upon it as a blessing of the gods.

The economy of life may have improved, after a few years, for the masses of Judah. The new puppet government, a low-level Babylonian administration in Mizpah, made less demands on their resources than the Davidic monarchy.

The modern bible student may get the impression that the devastation of Judah had been total. Verses like the following come to mind.

> I will wipe Jerusalem as one who wipes a dish, wiping it and turning it upside down. (2 Kgs 21:13)

Or we may recall the language of a covenant curse.

> ...the foreigner who comes from a distant country, will see the devastation of that land and the afflictions with which the Lord

has afflicted it—all its soil burned out by sulfur and salt, nothing
planted, nothing sprouting, unable to support any vegetation.
(Dt 29:22–23)

The first verse above is from the Jerusalem perspective only. And the curse
from Deuteronomy does not accurately describe what happened to the farm-
lands of Judah. The Babylonians did not destroy them in the fashion mentioned. The land was soon farmable, and some farmers owned their land for
the first time.[1] A passage in Jeremiah may be the tip of an iceberg related to
land reform that involved the breaking up of large, privately owned estates.[2]

Nebuzaradan the captain of the guard left in the land of Judah
some of the poor people who owned nothing, and gave them vine-
yards and fields at the same time. (Jer 39:10)

Religious Practices of the Masses of Judah During the Exile

We must remind ourselves that the great theological developments that were
taking place within the priestly communities of the Aaronids and the
Deuteronomists and that would become the great themes of the Hebrew bible
were completely unknown to the average Judahite. They had no way of knowing or comprehending the conflicting theologies developing within the
schools of the exiled priests. The people continued to worship several gods
and goddesses at high places and in family groups. The attempted reformation
of Josiah had reached some of the population. For the most part, however, it
was no longer applicable since the destruction of the temple and the deportation of the official priesthood.

We have many biblical references to the practices of religion in Judah
just before the final destruction of Jerusalem and also in postexilic writings.
An example of family practice is found in Jeremiah 7:18.

The children gather wood, the fathers kindle fire, and the women
knead dough, to make cakes for the queen of heaven.[3]

A remarkable conversation between Jeremiah and the women of Judah is
recorded for us in Jeremiah 44. The response of the women of Judah implies
that a reformation had partially taken place at some time in the recent past.

…But from the time we stopped making offerings to the queen of
heaven and pouring out libations to her, we have lacked everything and have perished by sword and famine. (Jer 44:18)

In a passage that many scholars identify as postexilic (Is 57:3–13),[4] we have references to ongoing practices condemned by both the torah of the Aaronids and the torah of the Deuteronomists. These practices include participation in sexual fertility rites, the slaughter of children, activities related to the dead (necromancy), the consulting of sorceresses and mediums, and the collecting of idols. In Isaiah 65 there are further references to sacrificing in gardens, offering incense on bricks and on mountains, and eating swine's flesh.

DIFFERENT MEANINGS FOR THE NAME ISRAEL

CHART 16

PROTO-ISRAEL: A heterogeneous grouping of subsistence-farming families and clans that emerged in the highlands of Canaan (from Dan to Beersheba), beginning around 1220 B.C.E. This Israel was rural without large cities or centralized government.

EARLY STATE OF ISRAEL: The political territory (nation-state) governed by David and Solomon from 1000 to 922 B.C.E.

THE NATION NORTH OF JUDAH: This nation-state, north of Judah (from Dan to Bethel), consisted of the territory whose people separated themselves from the house of David to form their own monarchy. This nation-state lasted for two hundred years, from 922 to 722 B.C.E.

ANOTHER NAME FOR JACOB: A northern tradition developed that presented the name Israel as an alternate name for the patriarch Jacob (Gn 32:28).

THE IDEALIZED PEOPLE OF YAHWEH: Israel became the name for a spiritualized, idealized people of Yahweh after the cessation of Judah as a nation-state (586) during and after the exile (Ezr 6:16). Judahites in Jerusalem and elsewhere (diaspora) saw themselves as Israelites, all descended from an idealized people who had had a common exodus experience, a Sinai/wilderness experience, and so forth. This is Israel of the bible as distinguished from Israel that produced the bible.

So the religion of rural Judah shared the characteristics of the religion of the surrounding areas. There are several corrections to be made to our thinking to sharpen our focus. (a) We should not think of the popular religion as only rural, practiced only by peasants. Jerusalemites had engaged in the same practices, and forms of popular religion were common in the temple from the time it was first constructed by Solomon. (b) Although some condemned practices may have been foreign in origin (such as astral worship from Assyria, including worship of the moon and the sun),[5] most of the practices condemned by the bible were not foreign or pagan in origin but were indigenous to Syria-Palestine, of which Israel was an integral part. (c) We sometimes get the idea that the inhabitants of Judah were ignoring Yahweh when they engaged in practices condemned by the two torahs.[6] This was not true. Yahweh was a major deity throughout Judah by the time of the exile, and many Judahites saw nothing contradictory in the worship of Yahweh along with other gods. One of the great contributions that the priestly torahs would make would be the establishment of one, and only one, God for Israel.

In reviewing the practices of religion in Judah during the exile, we should remember that we know of these practices only because the lofty, inspired theologians of the Aaronid priests and the Levitical priesthood (which traced its ancestry to Shechem) condemned them as incompatible with their high, majestic perceptions of Yahweh as the single god of Israel and their perceptions of the potential dignity of men and women, both declared to be created in the image of God. The theology of the two priesthoods, in some ways in constant tension, would be preserved for us in a collection of scrolls that would have an unimaginable influence on the course of human history. But as unique as the Hebrew bible turned out to be, it was the product of human beings with human failings, as we will see in the next chapter. God does move in mysterious ways.

NOTES

1. The Edomites had moved into the area south of Judah, but there was enough land left for the farmers of Judah.

2. A passage in Isaiah describes the grabbing of parcels of land by the rich to create large estates.

Ah, you who join house to house, who add field to field, until there is room for no one but you, and you are left to live alone in the midst of the land! (Is 5:8)

3. Susan Ackerman, in *Under Every Green Tree,* concludes that the queen of heaven was a syncretistic deity of west Semitic Astarte and east Semitic Istar. See pp. 5–35.

4. For a discussion of the dating of this passage, Isaiah 57:3–13, see Ackerman, *Green Tree,* pp. 111–16.

5. See Ezekiel 8:16–18, where Ezekiel has a vision of a form of astral worship:

> [There] were about twenty-five men, with their backs to the temple of the LORD, and their faces toward the east, prostrating themselves to the sun toward the east. (Ez 8:16)

And there are other references to worship of the heavens, such as the accusation that Manasseh built altars for all the host of heaven and served them in the temple (2 Kgs 21:3–4).

6. Biblical expressions, such as "they turned their backs to me" (Jer 2:27, 2 Chr 29:6); and passages in Hosea, such as "'Israel went after her lovers and forgot me,' says Yahweh" (Hos 2:13) and other expressions, give the impression that the people did not worship other gods at the same time that they worshiped Yahweh. This was not the case.

25

The Persian Period

The Persian period began in 539 B.C.E., when Cyrus issued an edict encouraging Judahites in Babylon to return to Jerusalem, and continued until the Greeks took over as the world power in 331. When I was a child and heard the story of the edict of Cyrus, I pictured the happy captives returning to Jerusalem to be greeted by cheering crowds of Judeans shedding tears of joy. Of course, when I became an adult I had to put away these naive thoughts. Consider the following:

(1) When Cyrus of Persia marched into Babylon, the captivity had lasted between forty-eight and fifty-eight years.

(2) While some of the original captives were still alive, the majority had been born in Babylon and had never seen Jerusalem.

(3) Jerusalemites whose families had not been taken into captivity did not look forward to the return of the exiles. There were several reasons for this, but one of them would have been related to possible ownership disputes concerning choice parcels of land that had been redistributed.

(4) Some captives in Babylon had become rich and comfortable and had no desire to return to Jerusalem.

(5) We know that some Babylonian Jews actually traveled in the opposite direction and moved to Persia! They made decisions to relocate in Persian cities and elsewhere, where there were cultural, educational, and economic opportunities.

(6) The world of Persian domination was a changing world. There were twenty satrapies divided into provinces stretching from Indus to the Danube, from Libya to Russia,[1] networked together with an improved road system, large seaports, and an official imperial language, Aramaic.

(7) Emigration from Babylon to Jerusalem started a long-lasting antag-
onistic division between immigrants (returnees) and natives.

(8) When a sufficient number of Babylonian Judahites arrived in
Jerusalem along with Aaronid priests, a process was initiated that
resulted in natives being looked on as second-class citizens.[2]

(9) The theology of the Aaronid priests, internalized by the returnees,
had convinced them that the natives of Jerusalem and the surrounding area were unholy and unclean.

(10) The decree of Cyrus may not have foreseen that one group of
Judeans would usurp the right to rebuild Jerusalem and the temple
from other people of Judah (Yehud).[3]

Ezra and Nehemiah

The very first governors of Yehud were probably related to or members of the
house of David. Zerubbabel is mentioned in Ezra (1–5), Haggai (1:12, 2:23), and
1 Chronicles 3:19. For a while a messianic hope was centered on Zerubbabel,
but his governorship ended in 515, the year that the second temple was completed, and nothing further is known of him. By the time the temple was rebuilt,
the house of David was out of the picture, and the priests were firmly in control.

After 515 the Greeks started to become a formidable enemy of Persian
domination, and early battles were joined. Almost a century had passed after
the edict of Cyrus when Ezra and Nehemiah were sent to Jerusalem[4] (between
460 and 440) to solve problems in the province.[5] It is good to remember that
both Ezra and Nehemiah were not Palestinian but Persian Jews.

There are several things we can learn from the book of Ezra. Although
Jews who had never been in captivity were considered unclean, there is an
indication that the natives of Judah, families that had not gone into captivity,
could become part of the holy, select community. A passover was held, and
natives were allowed to participate if certain conditions were met.

> It was eaten [the passover] by the people of Israel who had
> returned from exile, and also by all who had joined them, and sep-
> arated themselves from the pollutions of the nations of the land to
> worship the LORD, the God of Israel. (Ezr 6:2)

This tells us several important things: (a) A century after the first captives
returned to Jerusalem, the people who had returned from Babylon still considered themselves the select people of God. To institutionalize this belief,
Ezra established (reestablished) an official list of those who had returned
from captivity.

> Then my God put it into my mind to assemble the nobles and the
> officials and the people to be entered by genealogy. (Neh 7:5)

(b) The holiness laws and the characteristics of Judahite identity created by the
Aaronid priests during the captivity period were being observed, at least to
some degree. We are not told what the natives had to do to "...separate themselves from the pollutions of the nations of the land," but they may have been
the same things the captives had done to separate themselves from the people
of Babylon—keep the sabbath, circumcise their sons, observe dietary laws,
and participate in animal sacrifices and temple procedures, recognizing the
role of the temple priests in the holiness procedures. Perhaps observance of
yom kippur was also required.

Second Isaiah and the Aaronid Priests

Before we condemn the returnees for their apparent self-righteousness, there
are facts to be considered that will make us more sympathetic. The captivity
people, under the leadership of the Aaronid priests and under the teaching of an
impassioned exilic poet, had learned the meaning of the first commandment,

> I am the LORD your God, who brought you up out of the land of
> Egypt...you shall have no other gods before me. (Ex 20:2)

The exilic poet whom we know as Second Isaiah was a champion of the
Yahweh-only school (Is 43). This poet identified Yahweh with Elohim of
Genesis 1, using the Hebrew word for "create," *bara,* sixteen times. He had
attacked and ridiculed idolatry forbidden by the second commandment
(Is 41:29, 44:9–20, 47:6–7). He had been inspired by the rewritten exodus
story that had been fleshed out with detail from a scribe's knowledge of sixth-
century Egypt.[6] A new exodus for a new Israel, from Babylon, was the theme
of his inspired teaching.[7] He saw himself—and a spiritualized Israel—as a suffering servant of Yahweh (Is 42:1–7, 50:4–11, 50:4–9, 52:13–53:12). So it is
true that many of the returnees were changed people in possession of a new
Judahite identity because of the efforts of the Aaronid priests, the poet-teacher
(second Isaiah), and others whose names are not known to us. When the captives returned to Judah, they encountered a population that had not had the
benefit of five decades of purging.

The Popular Religion of the Postexilic Period

Third Isaiah is not a person but a collection of postexilic oracles. Two of these
oracles give us a picture of the popular religion of postexilic Judah, Isaiah

57:3–13 and 65:1–7. These oracles reveal to us a description of high-place activity involving child sacrifice, fertility-cult participation, necromancy, and hints of other activity condemned by the canonical scriptures.[8]

What happened to the popular religion of Israel and Judah? As time went on, it eventually passed into history along with the popular religion of other ancient cultures, Edomite, Moabite, Phoenician, Aramaean. While it is outside of the aim of this book to discuss the sociology of fading religions, it is good to keep in mind that the same fate would overtake the cults of super-powers like Egypt, Assyria, Chaldea, Greece, and Rome. Depending on their judgment, those who wrote and compiled the Hebrew bible avoided lengthy and specific references and descriptions of practices that were considered abominable to the holy one of Israel, the God who was emerging in Judah and among scattered communities of Judahites as the only God worthy of survival.

People of the Book

It is not our intention to carry our discussion into the period of canonization. We frequently read that when the theology of a dynamic religion is written in authoritative documents, the theology becomes frozen in time, institutional-ized as it were. This is not true. After the Hebrew scriptures were canonized, speculation, growth, lively debate, and dynamic growth continued. The Talmud came into existence, rabbinical writings and interpretations came into existence and multiplied, midrash developed. In the days of Jesus, there were many branches of Judaism—Sadducees, Pharisees, Zealots, the people of the land, and ascetic communities and their writings. This continued into the peri-ods of the church fathers, the reformation, and the counter-reformation. Throughout history, periods of interpretation of the scriptures varied in inten-sity, but today, on the verge of the twenty-first century, there are more schol-ars and students of the Hebrew bible than ever before. We have seen an expanding universe of biblical scholarship.

During the captivity period the scrolls became more precious to Judahites in Babylon and Egypt. Many more people learned to read in those cosmopolitan times. Scrolls were carried into all areas where the people of Israel found themselves. Eventually Jews were referred to as People of the Book. And the rest, as they say, is history.

There are a few loose ends we have to tie up in an epilogue.

NOTES

1. See Coote and Coote, *Power, Politics and the Making of the Bible*, pp. 74–78.

2. We have to remember the vision of Jeremiah concerning the good figs and rotten figs. The good figs were the Judeans taken into captivity, and the bad figs were the Judeans who were not taken into captivity. It causes one to wonder whether the whole passage concerning the figs was genuine with Jeremiah. After all, he and his friends and associates were not taken into Babylonian captivity. On the other hand, the rottenness that Jeremiah referred to may have been the temple and high-place practices of native Jerusalemites after the first captivity of 597. There is a similar passage in Ezekiel where the captives are declared blessed and the ones who remain behind are accused of abominations (Ez 11:14–21). But this we would expect from an Aaronid priest.

3. In Ezra we read these words attributed to Cyrus:
…and let all survivors in whatever place they reside, be assisted by the people of their place with silver and gold, with goods and animals, besides freewill offerings for the house of God in Jerusalem. (Ezr 1:2–4)
Also see ANET, p. 315.

4. Lemche, in his book *Ancient Israel,* says that Nehemiah arrived in Jerusalem in 445 B.C.E. and Ezra arrived around 398 B.C.E. To review the complexity of these dates, we recommend the article on Ezra and Nehemiah in the *New Jerome Biblical Commentary* by Robert North, S.J., pp. 384–86, and into the two commentaries.

5. There is an ongoing dispute among scholars concerning whether Ezra or Nehemiah arrived in Jerusalem first. For a thorough discussion of this problem and related matters, the reader is referred to the commentaries on Ezra and Nehemiah in the *NJBC*, pp. 384–98.

6. Donald B. Redford writes in *Egypt, Canaan, and Israel in Ancient Times* (Princeton, N.J.: Princeton University Press, 1992):
Whoever supplied the geographical information that now adorns the story [of the exodus] had no information earlier than the Saite period (seventh to sixth centuries B.C.). The eastern Delta and Sinai he describes are those of the twenty-sixth Dynasty kings and the early Persian overlords. (p. 409)

7. One of the priestly phrases is "Be fruitful and multiply." The scroll of Exodus begins by telling us "The Israelites were fruitful and prolific; they multiplied and grew exceedingly strong" (Ex 1:7).

8. There are some scholars who believe that the Isaiah passages cited here are exaggerations. Susan Ackerman, in *Under Every Green Tree,* states that the descriptions accurately describe popular cult practices of the late sixth century. Students are referred to chapters 3 and 4, pp. 101–217.

Epilogue

Our purpose in writing this text was to discover the religion of ancient Israel prior to the emergence of Judaism. Our starting point was the belief that Israel emerged in the highlands of Canaan late in the thirteenth century as a fragmented community of subsistence farmers. This was not the united Israel that entered a promised land under the leadership of Joshua after receiving the law from Moses or the Israel that was descended from the patriarchs and later was delivered from Egyptian bondage en masse. This is the Israel *of the bible,* not the Israel that produced the bible. It is important for serious students to understand both Israels.

We have used the scriptures of the Aaronids and the Deuteronomists as our primary sources for uncovering the outline of religious belief and practice in ancient Israel, keeping in mind the fact that these scrolls contained folklore, legend, myth, poetry, theology, lament, paean, prayer, and much more, frequently located in a chronological structure. There is a long story, and sometimes—in DH, for instance—the story comes close to history in the modern sense, presenting the overlapping reigns of the kings of Israel and Judah. The scribes of Judah belonged to one or another competing theological schools, and as it turns out, the viewpoints held by these schools complemented each other in interesting and valuable ways. It was the practice of the scribes of both the Aaronid priests and the Deuteronomists to re-create the past history of Israel and to project into that past theological truth as they understood it. Since both schools did the same thing, we have to assume that re-creating the past was the practice of the age and was considered an acceptable method of promoting one's viewpoint and teaching values to posterity. We cannot criticize them for what they did. We remember that our modern concepts of history are much different, but that the more we learn, the more we realize that the history our age produces is very subjective also.

Ancient Theologians

The scribes were more than theologians. Modern theologians study religion, both past and present, for academic reasons. Those ancient theologians were not mere academics but were persons of conviction and action committed to changing the behavior and understanding of their people and those who were yet unborn.

Levites

In the Tetrateuch and in the history of Chronicles, Levites are identified as temple assistants to the Sons of Aaron (Nm 18:1–4, for example). These assistants are not to be confused with the Deuteronomists who were descendants of the Levites of Shechem. As is often observed, in the book of Deuteronomy all priests were assumed to be Levites. In our book we frequently referred to the school that produced DH as the descendants of Shechemite Levites. In all cultures words can have several meanings, and in ancient Israel the word *Levite* was a generic word for priest for several centuries before the Tetrateuch appeared. They then became understood as priestly assistants.

What Happened to the Deuteronomists?

If Jeremiah and Baruch were part of the Deuteronomic circle, as we suspect, then we can trace the school to Egypt following the assassination of Gedaliah (Jer 43).[1] There is no doubt that during the exile the earlier Josianic version of DH was redacted, producing an exilic version emended to account for the destruction of Jerusalem and the temple by the neo-Babylonians (Chaldeans). The book of Deuteronomy and the scrolls of Hosea, Amos, Isaiah of Jerusalem, and Micah were also updated by the same circle during the exile.

The circle that produced the earlier, preexilic scrolls is called the Deuteronomic circle, and the exilic circle carries the title Deuteronomists. Numbered among the exilic Deuteronomists may have been older members of the preexilic school. During the exile the book of Deuteronomy was also expanded.[2]

We would love to have information concerning the role played by the Deuteronomists after the exile, but we have nothing but speculation. One of our guesses is that they were always small in number. They probably lost their identity as a school early in the postexilic period but not before delivering the canonical form of the scrolls in their collection.

The Pentateuch

We know that in the early postexilic period there were two scroll collections, the Tetrateuch of the Aaronids and the Deuteronomist collection. Deuteronomy (DH) and scrolls of the four eighth-century spokespersons who were later labeled prophets *(nabiim)* completed this collection. These two collections of scrolls represented the views of two diverse groups, but to what extent these two groups continued to be active in the restoration period we cannot say.

The royal priests who actually produced the Tetrateuch may have died in captivity, but their sons (also priests) returned to Yehud (the Persian name for Judah) with their newly created scrolls. The Persians had a policy of promoting an official body of law indigenous to the culture of the governed province. While there were two collections of scrolls to choose from in Yehud, the D collection was nationalistic and dwelt extensively on the throne of David. So the Tetrateuch became the Pentateuch by separating the scroll of Deuteronomy from the Deuteronomistic collection and adding it to the end of the Tetrateuch. The Pentateuch became the official torah of Yehud.[3] We stated earlier that the Aaronid law code was influenced by the book of Deuteronomy in several ways.

Had the Deuteronomists passed into history by the time the Pentateuch was created as the official code of Yehud? We cannot say for sure, but this is our assumption. Some scholars see some of the material in Third Isaiah as being related to the Deuteronomists. But Third Isaiah was influenced by several previous teachers who were no longer on the scene, including Isaiah of Jerusalem and Second Isaiah. A persuasive answer concerning the fate of the Deuteronomists is not available to us at this time.

The Period and Process of Canonicity

There are many fine books that describe the canonization process and period. Here are a few:

Joseph Blenkinsopp. *Prophecy and Canon.* Notre Dame, Ind.: University of Notre Dame Press, 1977.

Brevard Childs. *Old Testament Theology in a Canonical Context.* Philadelphia: Fortress Press, 1985.

John W. Miller. *The Origins of the Bible.* Mahwah, N.J.: Paulist Press, 1994.

James A. Sanders. *Torah and Canon.* Philadelphia: Fortress Press, 1972. Also, *Canon and Community.* Philadelphia: Fortress Press, 1984.

NOTES

1. Many scholars do not trace the Deuteronomists to Egypt.

2. See my book *Obsession with Justice: The Story of the Deuteronomists* (Mahwah, N.J.: Paulist Press, 1994).

3. We stated in a previous chapter that the torah of the Aaronids was influenced by Deuteronomy. The torah of the Aaronids started out as a manual for the priests and was expanded to include civil laws and to deal with justice issues peripherally. The royal priests learned many things from the Shechemite Levites.

For Further Reading

Ackerman, Susan. "The Queen Mother and the Cult in Ancient Israel." *SBL, Journal of Biblical Literature,* Fall 1993.

————. *Under Every Green Tree: Popular Religion in Sixth-Century Judah.* Atlanta: Scholars Press, 1992.

Aharoni, Yohanan. *The Land of the Bible.* Philadelpia: Westminster Press, 1979.

Ahlstrom, Gosta W. *The History of Ancient Palestine.* Minneapolis: Fortress Press, 1993.

Albertz, Rainer. *A History of Israelite Religion in the Old Testament Period.* Louisville, Ky.: Westminster/John Knox, 1994.

Barnes, William H. *Chronology of the Divided Monarchy.* Atlanta: Scholars Press, 1991.

Boadt, Lawrence. *Reading the Old Testament: An Introduction.* Mahwah, N.J.: Paulist Press, 1984.

Childs, Brevard. *The Book of Exodus.* Philadelphia: Westminster Press, 1974.

————. *Old Testament Theology in a Canonical Context.* Philadelphia: Fortress Press, 1985.

Clements, Ronald E. *The Cambridge Bible Commentary: Exodus.* Cambridge: Cambridge University Press, 1972.

Coote, Robert. *Amos Among the Prophets.* Philadelphia: Fortress Press, 1989.

————. *Early Israel.* Minneapolis: Augsburg/Fortress, 1990.

————. *In Defense of Revolution: The Elohist History.* Minneapolis: Fortress Press, 1991.

Coote, Robert, and Coote, Mary. *Power, Politics and the Making of the Bible.* Minneapolis: Fortress Press, 1990.

Coote, Robert, and Ord, David. *The Bible's First History.* Philadelphia: Fortress Press, 1989.

Coote, Robert, and Whitelam, K. "Social Scientific Criticism of the Hebrew Bible and Its Social World." *Semeia,* no. 37, 1986.

Craigie, Peter. *Deuteronomy*. Grand Rapids, Mich.: Eerdmans, 1976.

Cross, Frank Moore. *Canaanite Myth and Hebrew Epic*. Cambridge, Mass.: Harvard University Press, 1973.

Dearman, J. Andrew. *Religion and Culture in Ancient Israel*. Peabody, Mass.: Hendrickson, 1992.

Dever, William G. "How to Tell a Canaanite from an Israelite." *The Rise of Ancient Israel*. Washington, D.C.: Biblical Archaeology Society, 1992.

Doorly, William J. *Isaiah of Jerusalem: An Introduction*. Mahwah, N.J.: Paulist Press, 1992.

————. *Obsession with Justice: The Story of the Deuteronomists*. Mahwah, N.J.: Paulist Press, 1994.

————. *Prophet of Justice: Understanding the Book of Amos*. Mahwah, N.J.: Paulist Press, 1987.

————. *Prophet of Love: Understanding the Book of Hosea*. Mahwah, N.J.: Paulist Press, 1991.

Dozeman, Thomas. *God on the Mountain*. Atlanta: Scholars Press, 1989.

Eynikel, Erik. *The Reform of King Josiah*. Leiden: Brill, 1995.

Flanagan, J. W. "2 Samuel." *New Jerome Biblical Commentary*. Englewood Cliffs, N.J.: Prentice-Hall, 1990.

Friedman, Richard Elliot. *The Exile and Biblical Narrative*. Chico, Calif.: Scholars Press, 1981.

Gottwald, Norman K. *The Hebrew Bible, A Socio-Literary Introduction*. Philadelphia: Fortress Press, 1985.

————. *The Tribes of Yahweh*. Maryknoll, N.Y.: Orbis, 1979.

Hayes, John H., and Hooker, Paul K. *A New Chronology for the Kings of Israel and Judah*. Atlanta: John Knox Press, 1988.

Hopkins, David C. *The Highlands of Canaan*. Sheffield, U.K.: JSOT, 1985.

Houtman, Cees. "David and the Ark." *Journal of Biblical Literature*, Summer 1994.

Jagersma, H. *A History of Israel*. Philadelphia: Fortress Press, 1983.

King, Philip J. *Amos, Hosea, Micah—an Archaeological Commentary*. Philadelphia: Westminster Press, 1988.

Lemche, Niels Peter. *Ancient Israel*. Sheffield, U.K.: Academic Press, 1995.

Levenson, Jon D. *Sinai and Zion: An Entry into the Jewish Bible*. San Francisco: HarperCollins, 1987.

Mayes, Andrew D. H. *The New Century Bible Commentary: Deuteronomy*, Grand Rapids, Mich.: Eerdmans, 1979.

————. *The Story of Israel Between Settlement and Exile*. London: SCM Press, 1983.

Mays, James Luther, ed. *Interpreting the Prophets*. Philadelphia: Fortress Press, 1987.

McCarter, P. Kyle, Jr. "The Origins of Israelite Religion." *The Rise of Ancient Israel.* Washington, D.C.: Biblical Archaeology Society, 1992.

McKenzie, Steven L. *The Trouble with Kings.* Leiden: Brill, 1991.

Miller, John W. *The Origins of the Bible.* Mahwah, N.J.: Paulist Press, 1994.

Mullen, E. Theodore, Jr. *Narrative History and Ethnic Boundaries.* Atlanta: Scholars Press, 1993.

Nelson, R. D. *The Double Redaction of the Deuteronomistic History.* Sheffield, U.K.: JSOT, 1981.

Neumann J., and Parpola, S. "Climatic Change and the Eleventh–Tenth Century Eclipse of Assyria and Babylonia." *Journal of Near Eastern Studies* 46, 1987.

North, Robert, S. J. "Ezra and Nehemiah." *New Jerome Biblical Commentary.* Englewood Cliffs, N.J.: Prentice-Hall, 1990.

Noth, Martin. *Exodus.* Philadelphia: Fortress Press, 1962.

———. *A History of Pentateuchal Traditions.* Atlanta: Scholars Press, 1981.

Olyan, Saul. *Asherah and the Cult of Yahweh in Israel.* Atlanta: Scholars Press, 1988.

Porter, Joshua R. "Tabernacle." *Harper's Bible Dictionary.* San Francisco: Harper and Row, 1985.

Pritchard, James B. *The Ancient Near East,* Vol. 1. Princeton, N.J.: Princeton University Press, 1973.

Redford, Donald B. *Egypt, Canaan, Israel in Ancient Times.* Princeton, N.J.: Princeton University Press, 1992.

Shanks, Hershel, ed. *The Rise of Ancient Israel.* Washington, D.C.: Biblical Archaeology Society, 1992.

Smith, Mark S. *The Early History of God.* San Francisco: Harper and Row, 1990.

Spencer, John R. "Aaron." *Anchor Bible Dictionary.* New York: Doubleday, 1992.

Stern, Ephraim. "What Happened to the Cult Figurines?" *Biblical Archaeology Review,* July/August 1989.

Toorn, Karel van der. "David and the Ark." *Journal of Biblical Literature,* Summer 1994.

Van Seters, J. *In Search of History.* New Haven, Conn.: Yale University Press, 1983.

———. *The Yahwist as Historian.* Atlanta: Scholars Press, 1986.

Weinfeld, Moshe. *Deuteronomy and the Deuteronomic School.* Oxford: Clarendon Press, 1972.

Whitelam, K., and Coote, R. "Social Scientific Criticism of the Hebrew Bible and Its Social World." *Semeia,* no. 37, 1986.

Wolff, Hans W. *Joel and Amos.* Philadelphia: Fortress Press, 1984.

Yee, Gale. *Composition and Tradition in the Book of Hosea.* Atlanta: Scholars Press, 1987.

Subject and Author Index